Recent dramatic developments in China have increased Western interest in both her institutions and her politics. However, most of the studies dealing with the 'new' China tend to concentrate on recent events, leaving undocumented, particularly, the years between the establishment of the People's Republic in 1949 and the onset of the Cultural Revolution. To supplement this gap in the literature, Dr. Julia Kwong here examines the workings of a crucial institution—education—during this period in China's history.

The years from 1949 to 1966 saw swings from one educational policy to another, as proponents with differing views on how to achieve a true socialist state gained or lost ascendancy. The reciprocal key influence on each other of the economy and the educational system is Professor Kwong's focus. A deliberate attempt is made to evaluate critically the Chinese educational system in its cultural context, thus avoiding the pitfall of superimposing Western theoretical assumptions and biases on Chinese data.

Part I of the work details Chinese educational philosophy, the organization of the educational institutions, and the economic and social infrastructure established since 1949. Part II analyses the educational developments from the Great Leap Forward to the eve of the Cultural Revolution. The interaction between ideology, objective conditions, and power politics at both decision-making and implementation levels is discussed in detail, as are their various roles in shaping educational policy, and, consequently, the lives of the children concerned.

Dr. Kwong teaches sociology at the University of Manitoba.

CHINESE EDUCATION IN TRANSITION

Prelude to the Cultural Revolution

Julia Kwong

McGILL–QUEEN'S UNIVERSITY PRESS
MONTREAL

© McGill–Queen's University Press 1979
International Standard Book Number 0-7735-0341-2

Legal deposit third quarter 1979

Design by Hjordis P. Wills
Printed in Canada by John Deyell Company

This book has been published with the help of a grant from the Social
Science Federation of Canada, using funds provided by the Social
Sciences and Humanities Research Council of Canada

★ CONTENTS ★

★ TABLES ★

★ FIGURES ★

★ PREFACE ★

Recent educational development in China is one of the most neglected areas among the various studies of modern Chinese society. There are the collections of translations of documentary materials, invaluable to experts in the field, but perhaps too specific for many other readers. Interpretive accounts of Chinese educational changes may be more useful; a few of them deal with education since the establishment of the People's Republic of China, but most concentrate on the period after the Cultural Revolution. The years immediately prior to the Cultural Revolution are sadly neglected. More disconcerting to many social scientists, most of these studies analyse education in isolation, without relating it to the larger social context. Concepts and paradigms developed in the social sciences tend to be ignored in the analysis of Chinese data. One might expect that such studies would avoid the pitfall of superimposing western theoretical frameworks and biases on Chinese data. In fact, this is often not the case: biases *do* creep in; the values and assumptions of the authors are still there, merely relegated to the background.

This book tries to bring together a paradigm developed in the social sciences and the data on China. However, the theoretical framework used here is not a direct transplantation. To do so would be a betrayal of the dialectical materialism of my own intellectual root. The theoretical framework I employ is a synthesis of the Marxist paradigm with the analysis of Chinese reality. In putting forth the theoretical framework in the introductory chapter, the dual purpose of exposing my assumptions and values as well as providing guidelines to the reading of the book is served.

A second goal of this book is to supplement the time gap in the existing literature—hence its focus on the pre-Cultural Revolution period, particularly the years from the Great Leap Forward to the eve of the Cultural Revolution. My intention is to put the

revolutionary changes of the Cultural Revolution in a clearer perspective, thus enhancing our understanding of current developments in Chinese education. The data for the analysis are based
on both English and Chinese sources, supplemented by inter-
views with informants from and visitors to China.

A third goal is to study Chinese education in its social context.
The social milieu, however, is a complex whole, composed of a
number of intricate parts which defy thorough treatment in a
book of this length. I have therefore chosen the more limited one
of studying the relations of education to the economy, and the
mediating processes whereby the influences of the economy are
felt on education.

This book is written not only with the sophisticated scholar
(educators, sociologists, political scientists, and sinologists) in
mind; it is also addressed to the general interested reader and
students new to the field. Hence, every effort has been made to
make this book self-explanatory and self-sufficient. Part One provides the backdrop to the treatment of Chinese educational development: her educational philosophy, the organization of the
educational institutions, the economic and social infrastructures
since the establishment of the People's Republic of China. Part
Two analyses the educational developments from the Great Leap
Forward to the eve of the Cultural Revolution. It concentrates on
the interplay between the economy and education, and the interaction between ideology, objective conditions, and power politics
at both the decision-making and implementation levels in shaping educational outcomes. A list of suggested readings in the
English language is attached at the end of the book for any interested reader who might like to pursue the subject further.

★ACKNOWLEDGEMENTS★

Like any other piece of work, this one could not have been accomplished without the support and concerted efforts of a number of individuals and organizations. I am most grateful to Kazim Bacchus, who introduced me to the fields of sociology of education and development, and to David Livingstone for his incisive and constructive criticisms in the preparation of the manuscript. I am also grateful to Andrew Effrat, Paul Lin, Jack Wayne, and Donald Willmott for their advice and suggestions. To Ruth Sims I extend my appreciation for her unswerving attempts to improve the diction and flow of the manuscript, and to Trudy Baureiss, for the meticulous care with which she typed the draft at its various stages. In the preparation of the manuscript, I was helped by a grant from the University of Manitoba. The monthly seminars organized by the University of Toronto–York University Joint Centre on Modern East Asia in 1973–75 provided me with excellent exposure to prominent scholars in the field; they were a constant source of inspiration in the crucial formulating years of the manuscript.

Finally, I must express my gratitude to my husband, Victor. He has been the sounding board for my ideas; his insightful comments and continuing encouragement helped to make this book a reality.

CHINESE EDUCATION IN TRANSITION

★1★

Introduction

The educational system of the People's Republic of China, like her economic and political systems, has undergone tremendous changes over the past twenty-five years. However, studies of China's evolving educational system have lagged behind research into other aspects of her development, despite the substantial increase in the provision of education and marked changes in the structure of the system itself. True, with the opening of China to foreign visitors after the Cultural Revolution, numerous reports have been written on recent educational innovations, but these studies, with few exceptions, have overemphasized the innovativeness of reforms after the Cultural Revolution and have failed to recognize that the changes are really part of a continuous process.[1] None has attempted a systematic study of Chinese educational development in its social context.

In examining the relationship between the economy and education, most studies have concentrated on the supportive role of education in the economy, that is, on the relationship between investment in education and the consequent financial returns to the economy.[2] What they have tended to overlook is that the relationship is reciprocal: the state of the economy also affects educational development. Even in those few studies that do recognize the reciprocity of the relationship, the analysis is often presented within a functionalist framework—how the economy shapes educational development, or more specifically, how the economy facilitates educational development[3]—and it ignores the internal dynamics of the educational system which often result in a conflicting relationship between the economy and education.

In the following pages we explore the question of how education can develop within a social milieu that is itself in the process of change. The focus is on China in the period leading up to the

Cultural Revolution—a period characterized by the struggle of conflicting ideologies for dominance. In seeking to identify the dialectical influence of the economy on China's educational development, and also the contrary influences working within the educational system itself, it is my hope that some further light will be shed on the processes at work within any society in transition.

RELATIONSHIP BETWEEN EDUCATION AND ECONOMY

In undertaking any study, every social scientist has a theoretical perspective of society in mind, whether he acknowledges it overtly or not. While a theory specifying the relationship between two or more variables can be put to the test, a model of, or a theoretical perspective on society can be neither proven nor disproven. Nevertheless, the social scientist uses his theoretical perspective in the selection of problems, the organization of his ideas, and the pursuit of his inquiry.[4]

In the Marxist view, to which I subscribe, society is a 'social whole' composed of the economic substructure on the one hand, and the superstructure on the other. The economic substructure is looked on as the sum total of a society's productive relations, including not only man's relations to the productive forces, but also the social relations of the production process. It is the totality of these relations that constitutes the foundation of other spheres of society. The superstructure is seen as including institutions which fall into two broad categories: political-legal institutions and ideological ones. These institutions in general reflect tendencies in the underlying economic base and support the continuation of the status quo in the economic structure.[5]

One outgrowth of the Marxist conception of society is the view that the economic structure of society is the most important factor in bringing about social change. As the forces of production develop, the rate of production increases, making the existing social organization of production no longer compatible with the forces of production. This results in changes being introduced in the social relations of production to remove any fetters to the expansion of production. Elements in the superstructure which impede this full development are also modified or removed, so that as the economy changes, the other spheres of social conduct which make up the superstructure change in consequence.[6] Marxists view this relationship between the economic substructure and the superstructure as being far from mechanical. The economy is neither the only nor necessarily the most active element in shaping social change. Neither does the economy have an 'automatic' effect on the superstructure. While the different elements making up the superstructure depend on the economy for their existence, each of them has its own internal dynamics. They interact among themselves and in turn act on the economy. Engels analyses the respective roles of the different structures in the development of history in this way:

According to the materialist conception of history, the ultimate determining element in history is the production and reproduction of real life. More than this, neither Marx nor I have ever asserted. If, therefore, somebody twists this into saying that the economic element is the only determining one, he transforms that proposition into a meaningless, abstract, senseless phrase. The economic situation is the basis, but the various elements of the superstructure—political forms of the class struggle and its consequences, constitutions established by the victorious class after a successful battle, etc.—juridical forms—and even the reflexes of all these actual struggles in the brains of the participants: political, legal, philosophical theories, religious ideas and their further development into systems of dogmas—also exercise their influence upon the course of the historical struggles and in many cases preponderate in determining their form.[7]

In other words, social change is not determined solely by changes in the economic structure. It is also modified by specific conditions in a particular social historical context.

This conjoint effect of specific conditions is further elaborated by Marxists like Louis Althusser, who maintains that the general direction of development is modified by existing conditions within a society acting as a whole at a particular point in time. The interplay of the different influences and their relative strength in both the substructure and the superstructure results in the specificities of each situation. He defines the concept of overdetermination as follows:

The unity they [contradictions in the superstructure and the economic base] constitute in this 'fusion' into a revolutionary rupture, is constituted by their own essence and effectivity, by what they are, and according to the specific modalities of their action. In constituting this unity, they reconstitute and complete their basic animating unity, but at the same time, they also bring out its nature: the 'contradiction' is inseparable from the total structure of the social body in which it is found, inseparable from its formal conditions of existence, and even from the instances it governs; it is radically affected by them, determining but also determined in one and the same movement, and determined by the various levels and instances of the social formation it animates; it might be called overdetermined in its principle.[8]

The above quotation introduces another point in the Marxist analysis of social development: the role of contradiction and conflict in the process of change. Marx perceives the development of history as a process of class struggle:

The history of all hitherto existing societies is the history of class struggle. Free man and slave, patrician and plebian, lord and serf, guild master and journeyman, in a word, oppressor and oppressed, stood in constant opposition to one another, carried on an uninterrupted, now hidden, now open fight, a fight that each time ended in a revolutionary reconstitution of society at large or in the common ruin of the contending class.[9]

Marxists see this conflict among classes as being rooted in the property relationship in the economic structure. Members of the ruling class, through their control of the economy, also control the superstructure which supports their interests. In the process, they appropriate the surplus value of production, reduce the workers to a subordinate position, and polarize society into two classes, the oppressor and the oppressed. While class conflict is based on the distribution of power in the economic base, these conflicts find expression in the superstructure and are most intense in the political arena.

The Marxist model of social change offers several useful guidelines in the analysis of the relationship between the economy and educational development. It helps us both to situate the economy and education within the larger social framework and to recognize not only the importance of the economic structure in determining educational development, but also the specific social and historical context in which interaction between economy and education takes place. This emphasis on conflict as an ever-present reality in the social milieu, sensitizes one to the contradictions that might exist between the economy and the various parts of the superstructure.

Despite their emphasis on the dialectical aspect of the relationship between the substructure and the superstructure, Marx and Engels, in their preoccupation with defending the main principle, the primacy of the economy vis à vis their adversaries, have not examined this relationship in great detail. Neither have they analysed the relationship between the economy and education in particular. This gap in the Marxist framework is to a certain extent bridged by the theories of Althusser, Carnoy, Lefebvre, and Poulantzas.

Supportive Relationships between the Economy and Education
According to Marx, the economic system regenerates itself through the system of exchange and other processes that go on within the economy. The proletarian sells his labour to the capitalist and takes part in the production process. In turn, he buys back the products of his own labour from the capitalist. Through this process of exchange, the exploitation of the proletariat by the capitalists continues.[10]

While Althusser agrees that the economy tends to regenerate itself, he maintains that it also perpetuates its existence through a variety of other means. The state apparatus, for example, contributes to the maintenance of the economy through its control over the process of production and its intervention on behalf of the ruling class. The repressive state apparatus, which includes the military and the police, protects the interests of the ruling class through coercion and the threat of physical force. For example, the police may intervene to put down worker unrest. The ideological state apparatus, which includes organized religion and the educational system, serves the same end through the propagation of an ideology supportive of the existing structure.[11] In the case of education, its major role is to supply a given number of individuals with sufficient training to maintain or increase production. This training includes not only the inculcation of the specific cognitive or manual skills necessary for a specific job, but also, Carnoy adds, education in the values and attitudes that sustain the existing social and political order.[12] In other words, the role of the school is to provide the necessary mental, physical, and ideological training necessary for the maintenance of the economic status quo.

This supportive relationship between the economy and education, identified by Althusser and Carnoy, can be further clarified by breaking down the components of education and specifying the linkages between the two structures more clearly. According to Marx, the economy is composed of the forces of production, the social relations of production, and most important, the property relations of production. This framework, used by Marx in the analysis of the economy, can be extended to education. Education, like the economy, does not refer only to such measurable indices as the number of schools and enrolment; it includes a whole set of structural relationships, the most important of which is the intrinsic internal power relationship. Education serves the class interests of those who control it. If we can identify the class bases of the holders of power at both the policy-making and the implementation level, we can predict the nature of the educational system, whom it is to serve, and the kind of education that will be provided. The second element to be considered is the curriculum. This takes in what is taught in the schools: the theoretical/technical knowledge and attitudes, and the relative importance placed on each. The former is influenced by the forces of production in the economic base, the latter by the ideology of the policy-makers and the implementers. The third component is the social relationship of education—how it is organized. Included here is the administration of the schools and the question of whether the system is elitist or open. Often the administration of the school, whether it is centralized or decentralized, bears a close resemblance to the authority structure in the workplace. In examining the role that the economic structure plays in determining educational development, we see that the economic substructure asserts an influence on education not only in selecting who controls it and whom it is to serve, but also in deciding the curriculum and the way the system is organized. These supportive relationships are schematically represented in Figure 1.

Figure 1. **Supportive Relationship between
Economic Substructure and Educational Development**

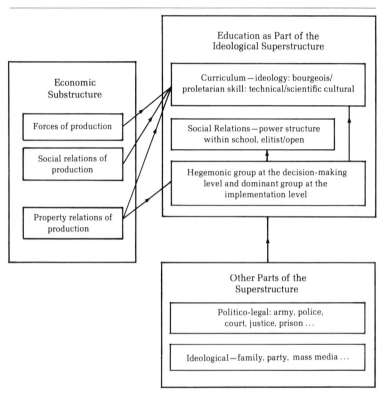

* The arrows indicate the paths of direct relationship only.

Contradictory Relationships
between the Economy and Education

While the relationship between the economy and education is close, it is not necessarily mutually supportive. Althusser's and Carnoy's concept of the educational system as an ideological state apparatus may help to explain the supportive role of education in the reproduction of the economic structure and be adequate in capturing the dominant trend in a period when a particular mode of production is entrenched. Their concept may even be suited to Carnoy's analysis of the neo-colonial period, when the political power of the colonizer in the newly independent state was replaced by the power of an indigenous group which maintained close commercial and cultural ties with the mother country, patterning the economy of the new state on the lines of the one that spawned it. In the neo-colonial period, though there was a change in political power, there was no fundamental change in the class basis of that power. The educational system remained supportive of the capitalist system. However, in a period of transition which involves a fundamental change in the economic base, the relationship between the economy and education can be contradictory because of the resilience of older structures and their ability to perpetuate themselves. In *Grundrisse*, Marx analyses this phenomenon in the development of capital:

> Money becomes capital as a result of prerequisites, namely the possession of real conditions for the creation of new values without exchange—through its own process of production. These prerequisites, which are originally conditions of its formation ... now appear as the result of its own realization, its own reality, as established by it—not as the condition of its coming into being, but as the result of its existence. Capital no longer proceeds from prerequisites in order to develop; it is its own prerequisite, and proceeds from itself, creating the presuppositions of its maintenance and growth.[13]

As the institution of capital acquires strength, it develops not only on the basis of the old structures which spawned it, but on the basis of itself; it moves according to its own laws.

Both Althusser and Carnoy inadvertently overlook the implication of this tendency of the social system to reproduce itself, but Lefebvre engages in lengthy discussion of its implication.[14] A system, once started, acquires its own dynamics and tends to perpetuate itself. In the process of societal change, not all structures are transformed at the same rate; some are, but others exhibit strong resistance to change. Lefebvre compares society at any particular juncture to 'a jumble of differently dated pieces offering inscriptions, many of them worn out'. Poulantzas, in his analysis of the state,[15] also shows that while societies at any point in history may be dominated by a particular mode of production, be it feudal, capitalist, or socialist, none exists in an unalloyed form. Instead, they co-exist with traits from other modes of production and structures. Characteristics of these different modes of production can be found in both the superstructure and the economic base. Within the state apparatus, it results in a 'dislocation', or lag, between the repressive state apparatus and the ideological one.[16]

The theories of Marx, Lefebvre, and Poulantzas can be pursued further. The requirements and needs of any two modes of production are never entirely compatible; often they are at odds with each other and, in the process, create conflict within the substructure and the superstructure. Neither of these structures or sets of structures are isolated entities; they vie for one another's support to reproduce themselves, and thus generate not only a supportive relationship between themselves but also an element of conflict among their individual parts which support different modes of production. The relationship between the economy and education is, therefore, potentially both supportive and contradictory. In its attempt to support the emerging mode of production in the economic base, the educational system may be working against the mode of production from which it arises.

To capture this dialectical aspect of the relationship, clear specification is necessary. Distinctions have to be made between different modes of production (feudal, capitalist, or socialist) co-existing within the economic base and the different types of superstructure that arise from or support them. Figure 2 shows how the contradictory and supportive aspects in the relationship between the economy and education in China might be expressed. In China, the property relationship in the economic base has been largely transformed into a socialist one, but the educational system has retained strong capitalist tendencies. As a result, the predominantly socialist economic system demands that the educational system support socialism, while the educational superstructure,

Figure 2. Economic Substructure and Educational Development

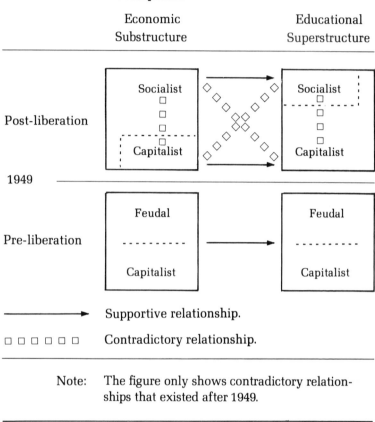

Supportive relationship.

□ □ □ □ □ □ Contradictory relationship.

Note: The figure only shows contradictory relationships that existed after 1949.

which still contains many traits of the capitalist social formation,
tends to resist, and continues to support the remnants of the capitalist economy.[17]

MEDIATION PROCESS BETWEEN
ECONOMY AND EDUCATION

Our next question is: How does the economic structure influence
the educational structure? Again, we have to refer to the works

of later Marxists to identify the more significant paths of the mediation between the two structures. The works of Lenin, Miliband, and Poulantzas[18] do not deal directly with the dynamics of educational development or the relationship between the economy and education. However, Lenin's and Poulantzas' attempts to develop a theoretical framework for understanding the relations between the economic base and the state, and Miliband's analysis of this relationship in British society, throw some light on the question.

Like Marx, Poulantzas and Lenin hold that the relations of production in the economic base determine to a large extent the formation of social classes in a society, and their relative dominance or subjection. Lenin observes that because of the existence of the different classes and factions within a society, with their conflicts of interest, the state emerges as the arbitrator:

> The state is ... by no means a power forced on society from without ... rather it is a product of society at a certain stage of development. It is the admission that this society has become entangled in an insoluble contradiction with itself, that it has split into irreconcilable antagonisms. But in order that these antagonisms, these classes with conflicting economic interests might not consume themselves and society in fruitless struggles, it became necessary to have a power, seemingly standing above society, that would alleviate the conflict and keep it within the bounds of order.[19]

The state is, in effect, an organ of class rule whereby one class, usually the dominant class in the economic system, exerts power over another. The dominant class tries to create an order which legalizes and perpetuates existing social relations of production by moderating the conflicts among classes. It derives its mandate from its superior position within the economic and the political structures, and through its control of state power it also controls the ideological state apparatus that ensures the acceptance of its hegemony.

As was noted earlier, at any point in a society's history, the dominant mode of production often co-exists with traits from other modes of production. Poulantzas shows that the economy in early nineteenth-century Britain was characterized by outgoing agrarianism and incoming industrialization. The dominant class in the political structure was, in fact, an alliance of the different sectors that made up the dominant class in the economy—the landed aristocracy and the rising bourgeoisie—but the landed aristocracy held the leading position. In other words, the landed aristocracy was the hegemonic group; that is, it not only represented the class that dominated the economic base, it held the leading position among the different factions within the political apparatus. Through its control of the state power, says Poulantzas, the hegemonic group provides the guidelines for assessing objective conditions, defines needs and priorities, and formulates the policies of the state in the interests of the dominant class in the economy, even though the state apparatus is not necessarily occupied by the same incumbents. This accounts for the supportive relationship between the economy and the state apparatus.

While the hegemonic group may control state power and provide the ideological base for its functioning, Poulantzas observes that it does not necessarily provide the manpower for the bureaucracy. This is usually recruited from a subordinate stratum; for example, in a capitalist society, it usually comes from the petty bourgeoisie. The recruitment of the bureaucracy from a lower stratum does not arise out of the need of the hegemonic class for alliance to bolster its power, but rather from the weakness of the subordinate stratum, which requires representation through the bureaucracy 'because of the economic conditions of life [e.g., isolation, etc.] and the incapacity of the class of small scale producers politically to organize themselves'.[20] Later, Poulantzas develops his ideas further and makes the distinction between the upper and lower echelons of the bureaucracy. While the recruitment of the bureaucracy at the lower level remains independent of class origins, the recruitment of the upper echelons represents a strategy of alliance and compromise among the groups striving for dominance. In late nineteenth-century Britain, he notes, the bourgeoisie had become the hegemonic group, but the personnel in the higher levels of administration was still supplied by the landed aristocracy it had supplanted. At the lower levels, the bourgeoisie remained the pliant tool of the administration.[21]

A similar position is taken by Miliband in his analysis of government in a capitalist sytem.[22] Even though different political parties may dominate the state apparatus at different periods, they share dominance in relation to the economic structure. The government may change hands among the different political parties, but the basic policy guidelines do not change. The differences among the political parties are no more than contradictions among the dominant class, as opposed to the antagonisms that exist between the exploiters and the exploited. The bureaucracy within the state apparatus remains relatively stable. It represents the petty bourgeoisie, who share the ideology of the dominant class. The hold of the petty bourgeoisie on the state apparatus further contributes to the stability of capitalism within the state apparatus.

The theories of Poulantzas and Miliband contribute much to our understanding of the relationship between the economy and education, because they identify the agents that control the ideological state apparatus at both the decision-making and the implementation levels. The hegemonic group that controls the economic structure and the state apparatus also dominates the educational system. It provides the guidelines for the policies and the direction for educational development. Poulantzas' and Miliband's analysis of the composition of the bureaucracy also has implications for our understanding of educational development, not only as to how its policies are implemented, but also to what extent. In hypothesizing that the agents of the bureaucracy are a willing tool of the dominant class, Poulantzas and Miliband underplay the contradictions between the hegemonic group and the bureaucracy, giving the impression that the policy guidelines of the class in power generally go unopposed at the lower level.

Marx's concept of ideology has to be introduced at this point to understand the extent to which Poulantzas and Miliband underrate the contradiction between the decision-making and the implementation levels. Marx did not use his concept of ideology to explain social development; however, it can be extended to explain the paths of mediation between the economy and education, and especially the conflicting relationship between the two structures in a period of transition.

Ideology is not just a conceptual scheme, says Marx. It is the 'superstructure of another structure'; 'it is the terrain on which men move, acquire consciousness of their position, struggle.'[23] In other words, men make decisions for their actions within the confines of their ideology.

While not discounting man's capacity for independent action and his ability to transform social existence, Marx holds that man's ideology or social consciousness is shaped by his social existence, and particularly, by those activities related to production. 'The mode of production of material life conditions the general process of social, political and intellectual life. It is not the consciousness of men that determines their existence, but their social existence that determines their consciousness.'[24] Moreover, states Marx, man's ideology is not static. Because his activities bring him into constant interaction with social reality, his ideology, which arises out of his social existence, is constantly being challenged and changed. This provides the framework by which he perceives reality and decides on his course of action, but the effect of his action on social reality in turn modifies and shapes his ideology.

Ideology provides the mediating link in our analysis of the relationship between the economic and the educational structures. The ideology of the hegemonic group provides the framework and guidelines by which the group assesses, not only existing economic conditions and their requirements, but also educational conditions, the demands of the economic structure, and the priorities to be given to various types of educational development. The educational policies, once formulated, adopted, and implemented, act on the objective conditions, and in turn tend to modify or reinforce the ideology or outlook of the hegemonic group. It is this dynamic process that leads the hegemonic group to decide whether existing policies are to be continued or changed. This explains the supportive links between the economy and education.

More importantly, Marx's conception of ideology helps us to explain the contradictions between the economic substructure and the educational superstructure. In a period of transition from capitalism to socialism, the ideology of the masses has its roots in the capitalist social formation, even though the structure of the economic base has been largely transformed. In the early stages of transition, at least, the prevailing ideology of the populace carried over from the capitalist era still retains capitalist traits. For example, when the hegemonic groups involved want to create an educational system more suitable to socialist construction, many of their teachers still prefer the traditional academic educational system. These differences of perception inevitably give rise to conflict between the implementers and the decision-makers. Because of their different ideologies, the implementers often act contrary to state policies. As Lenin pointed out with respect to Russia after the revolution, 'the old officials ... from the tsar and from the bourgeois society ... partly deliberately and partly unwittingly' worked against the new regime and perpetuated the old system.[25]

The presence of traditional elites in the bureaucracy of a society in transition certainly does not represent a strategy of alliance in the sense that Poulantzas suggests: the traditional elite tends to remain antagonistic to the ideology of the hegemonic group who, having only recently gained control of the state apparatus, is dependent on their services. This provides members of the traditional elite with the opportunity to retain their power in the bureaucracy—within the limitations set by the ideology and control of the hegemonic group. It is important to recognize the existence of this contradiction between the hegemonic group and the bureaucracy because it explains to a large extent the survival of capitalist traits within the new state structure and thus the contradictions between the economy and education.

This point underlines the weakness in Miliband's and Poulantzas' analyses of the bureaucracy. Miliband concentrates his analysis on a period when a particular mode of production is strongly entrenched. Consequently, he interprets the bureaucracy as an important stabilizing element within the capitalist political system. Similarly, while Poulantzas' conceptualization of the bureaucracy as a pliant tool of the hegemonic group may be adequate for the European societies he analyses, where the petty bourgeoisie shares essentially the same ideology as the hegemonic group, it is not applicable to a society in transition where the positions of the dominated and the dominator have been reversed and revolution is carried out by the vanguard.

There are not only differences of opinion between the hegemonic group and the implementers in a period of transition, there are also differences of opinion within both the hegemonic group and the bureaucracy. Again we have to refer to Marx's dialectical conception of ideology; this is because no two persons have identical experience and a consequent identical ideology. Even among the hegemonic group, differences of opinion on the priorities assigned to the different aspects of development and strategies of development can always be found; the process of policy formulation at the national level is not devoid of contradictions and conflict. And, in a period of transition, when the ideology of the incumbents develops not only on the basis of the existing social formation, but also has its roots in the old, greater diversities of opinion occur. When membership in the hegemonic group is often limited to those who share 'similar' ideologies, membership in the lower echelons is less restricted. Consequently, diversities are even more pronounced at the implementation level between the traditional holders of power and the supporters of the new hegemonic group.

Power relationships is therefore an important variable operating in the dialectics of educational development. Given differences of opinion among the agents, the adoption of policies at the decision-making level depends on the support each faction is able to muster, and that is a function of two things: the sharing of a similar ideology, and the perceived efficacy of the policies (before and after their implementation) in solving existing problems. The members of the hegemonic group may share the basic goals of the new society; however, they may not agree on the set of priorities or strategies of development. Moreover, while one's ideology is a more or less consistent and an organized system of thought, the evaluation of policy results is open to interpretation. Often this divergence of opinion results in a shift in the balance of power among the hegemonic group, especially after a set of policies is in effect for some time. Depending on the stability of the balance of power among these different factions, there may be swings of the pendulum from one set of policies to another and back. Indeed, many sinologists have seen this shifting power balance as the variable to explain the fluctuations in Chinese policies.[26] However, in so doing, they have overlooked the complexities of the situation that we have discussed earlier.

The shift of alliance is not necessarily a smooth process; it may be accompanied by intense negotiations, lobbying, and conflict. In the Chinese case, information on what actually took place before the Cultural Revolution is not available. The existence of conflict only became apparent when the struggle got so intense that it could not be resolved through negotiation or compromise and resulted in the open purging of the key members. This resolution, however, indicated only that one faction had gained dominance. Later, during the Cultural Revolution, when the masses were

Figure 3. Mediation Process between Economic Substructure and Educational Development

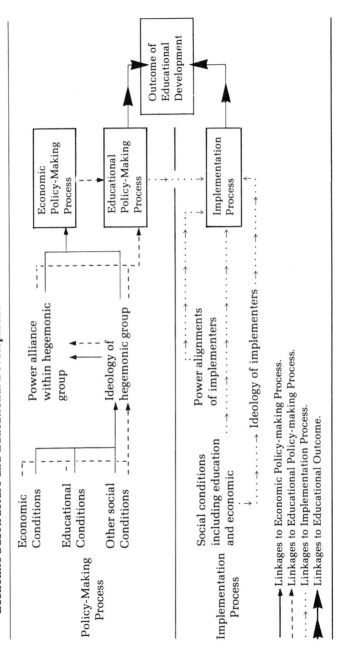

involved in the power struggle between two lines of development, both the delicate balance of power and the struggle were more easily detectable. In looking to the years before the Cultural Revolution, however, we have to be content with identifying differences through the outcome alone, rather than through watching the manner in which the differences were resolved.

The outcome of educational development depends as much on the policies formulated as on the manner in which they are implemented. While it is true that policy directives are generally defined at the centre, the bureaucracy is empowered to implement them. To run the risk of being unduly repetitious, it is worth reiterating that the variables mentioned earlier, ideology and power relationships, are as pertinent to the decision-making process as to the implementation process. The ideologies of the implementers and the power relationships within this group also have to be taken into consideration. The working of these two variables in the implementation process can have an important influence not only on the success or failure of the policies, but, as well, on the outcome of these policies which, ultimately, shape new policies coming from the centre.

The mediation process between education and the economy is represented in Figure 3. The mediating links rest on the ideologies of the agents involved in the educational process, the ways they perceive the requirements of economic and educational conditions, the balance of power among the decision-makers and the implementers, and the actions they take after assessing objective conditions.

This theoretical framework is essentially based on the works of Marx, Lenin, Lefebvre, Miliband, and Poulantzas. With the possible exception of Lenin, the works of these social scientists are oriented towards the study of capitalist societies. The one developed here is more geared towards the study of societies in transition to communism, that is, socialist societies. In the following pages, we shall apply it to the analysis of the development of education in China. However, it needs to be pointed out that the following analysis is not, nor does it claim to be, an exercise in hypothesis-testing; data are too limited to allow the degree of rigour required in such an exercise. Rather, the aim is to use this framework to clarify the dynamics of recent Chinese educational development.

PART ★ ONE

*Socio-Economic Background
of Chinese Educational
Development*

★2★

Social Groups
in Chinese Education

In the years before the communists came to power in 1949, the Chinese economy was both feudal and capitalist. The basis of the economy was agriculture. Over 85 percent of the population engaged in farming, and about 70 percent of the land under cultivation was owned by the landlords, though they constituted only 10 percent of the population. The peasants were usually either rentiers or hired labourers on the landlords' farms. On the other hand, most of the large industries that grew up along the coast were under foreign control, while smaller factories were in the hands of the bourgeoisie.[1]

In 1949, when the communists took over political power, the process of transferring private property to the state began. By 1956, the take-over of private property was essentially complete, rendering the economic criterion (the ownership of property) for social class inadequate. But the historical effects remained. Class distinctions continued to exist, even after liberation, but with one notable difference: it was now ideology, and not so much the actual possession of economic power, that divided Chinese society into different social classes.

In 1958, Liu Shao-ch'i analysed the composition of Chinese society in this way:

> There are two exploiting classes and two labourer classes in Chinese society today. One of the exploiting classes comprises the bourgeois rightists who oppose socialism, the landlord and compradore classes whose rule had been overthrown, and other reactionaries. The bourgeois rightists are to all intents and purposes agents of the imperialists, the remnants of feudal and compradore forces and Chiang Kai-shek's KMT [Kuomintang or Nationalist Party]. The other exploiting class comprises the national bourgeoisie and their intellectuals who are accept-

ing socialist transformation step by step. Most of them are in a state of transition wavering between the socialist road and the capitalist road. One of the labouring classes comprises the peasants and other labourers who formerly worked on their own. The overwhelming majority of these have joined cooperatives and are becoming increasingly enthusiastic supporters of socialism. The other is the working class, the most advanced contingent of the whole people and the leading force in our state power and the cause of socialism. All these four categories of people have undergone tremendous changes in the course of the rectification campaign and the anti-rightist struggle.[2]

The criteria by which the party identified a person as either bourgeois or a member of the proletariat did not rest to any great extent on his possession of the means of production. It rested on his family background as it existed before liberation and on his ideology as it related to the acceptance of socialism. Even though the ownership of property may have ceased to exist, it remained one of the criteria of identification because the ideologies of the different classes remained, although they took various forms. 'Even if the bourgeoisie as a class has disappeared economically, the bourgeois world outlook, the political influence of the bourgeoisie, and the forces of bourgeois and petty bourgeois habits will continue to exist for a long time in conflict with the socialist system.'[3]

The Chinese government accepted that an individual could transcend his class origins through ideological remoulding. A person coming from a landlord or capitalistic background would naturally be more exposed to bourgeois influences, and more likely to be bourgeois in ideology and way of life, but he could become 'progressive'. At the same time, a person with a working-class background could also serve bourgeois interests. As the society moved towards socialism, the Chinese government accepted that a person's ideology, combined with his behaviour, became the dominant criteria for determining his class. 'According to the Marxist viewpoint of class struggle, the most important way of judging a representative of a particular class is to see the line and policies he pushes and the interest of the class he represents.'[4]

This definition of a person's class position is in keeping with the Marxist interpretation of the dialectics involved in the formation of a person's ideology, which, to a great extent, is determined by his objective existence, especially by his position in relation to the means of production. However, because of the unique combination of social, economic, and political events, individual experiences, and the dialectics of the relationship between ideology and objective conditions, not all those coming from similar economic backgrounds share the same ideology. Also, variations in the ideology of individuals coming from similar class backgrounds are likely to be greater in a period of transition, when a person's ideology is shaped not only by the class background he was born into, but also by the dramatic changes in the economic substructure and his individual reaction to these changes. Since property ownership is rendered obsolete in the socialist era, the only valid way of assessing a person's class position is through examining his actions and seeing with which class he most closely identifies.

The revolutionary vanguards of the 1940s were not necessarily Marxists. In 1946, only one million out of a population of 460 million belonged to the Communist Party.[5] While some saw the Communist Party as a viable alternative to Chiang Kai-shek's Nationalist Party, the KMT, in uniting China and resisting Japan, others were spurred on by a spirit of nationalism and were influenced by western ideologies of liberation and democracy. Even within the party, some of its members were not fired by any real understanding of Marxism. In 1951, Liu Shao-ch'i analysed the composition of the Communist Party thus:

> The people joining our Party not only differ in class origin and personal class status but also carry with them aims and motives of every description. Many of course, join the Party in order to bring about communism and attain the great goal of emancipation of the proletariat and all mankind, but some do for other reasons and with other aims. For example, some comrades of peasant background used to think that communism meant 'expropriation of local tyrants and distribution of land'. Today quite a number of people join the Party chiefly because it is resolute in resisting Japan and advocates the

National United Front against Japan. Others join our ranks because they admire the Communist Party for its good reputation or because they realize in a vague way that it can save China. Still others are seeking a future for themselves, because they have no other way out—they have no fixed occupation, are out of work, lack the means to study, or want to escape from family bondage or forced marriage, etc. A few even join because they count on the Party to have their taxes reduced or because they hope to make their mark some day, or because their relatives or friends have brought them in.[6]

The fact that the Communist Party represented only a minority of the population and was composed of members of dubious intentions had important repercussions on the educational structure after liberation.

For one thing, it was impossible to recruit into the educational bureaucracy only party members or those who shared the communist ideology. While the total membership of the Communist Party (CCP) had risen to about 10 million by 1956, only 3.8 percent, that is 400,000, of its members were engaged in education and cultural work.[7] The total engaged in education throughout the country is not known, but judging from the small number of party members engaged in cultural work, they were probably in the minority. Even among this group, the members' commitment to socialist construction could not be absolutely certain.

While it may be that the CCP dominated the policy-making level in the educational system after 1949, it would have been impossible for it to have done so at the implementation level. Its personnel had to have a certain level of education or training, and among the Communist Party members, only 12 percent were classified as intellectuals; 83 percent still belonged to the worker and peasant classes.[8] In the years immediately after liberation, many of the personnel in the educational system were holdovers from the nationalist regime—not too surprising, considering that the majority of the educated belonged to the traditional elites (landlords and bourgeoisie) who had monopolized the provision of education before liberation. In a study of the faculty members of Peking University in the fifties, Greenblatt found that 90.8 percent had received their education before liberation, and most had been working in the university before 1949.[9] It seems likely that

Table 1   Social Background of Members of the
Chinese Communist Party in 1956-57

	1956		1957	
	Percentage	Number	Percentage	Number
Worker-peasant	83.1	8,920,273	80.5	10,240,000
Intellectual	11.7	1,255,923	14.8	1,880,000
Other	5.2	558,188	4.7	600,000

Source: John W. Lewis, *Leadership in Communist China* (Ithaca:
Cornell University Press, 1963), p. 108.

these persons were affected by their socialization before liberation, and did not accept the ideology of the Communist Party.

A crude index in determining a person's position in relation to
the organization of Chinese education is whether he was more
involved in policy-making or in implementation. Even though the
ideology of the ruling class emphasized the common good, and
sectarian or narrow professional interests were frowned upon,[10]
divisions between the policy-making and implementation levels
did exist, and they must be distinguished because these divisions
defined a person's role in the educational process. There was
also a tendency for Communist Party members to dominate the
decision-making level and for non-communists or traditional
elites to occupy the implementation level.

Class position is another important criterion to be considered.
A person's ideology, the class interests he represented, influenced
the decisions he made, the factions he supported. At the implementation level, even though the actions of the cadres (administrative personnel) were circumscribed by directives from the
centre, these directives provided only general guidelines. Details
were worked out at the implementation level, and a person's
ideology would exert an influence on the strategies he chose and
the way he interpreted policies.

Within the Chinese educational system, one can use these criteria to identify four different social groups:

(1) policy-makers with a proletarian outlook;
(2) policy-makers with a bourgeois outlook;

(3) implementers with a proletarian outlook;
(4) implementers with a bourgeois outlook.

POLICY-MAKING LEVEL (GROUPS 1 AND 2)

The direction of educational development was formulated at the National People's Congress (NPC). When the congress was not in session, its functions were taken over by the Standing Committee of the NPC. The highest administrative organ was the State Council, assisted by the Office of Education and Culture. Under it, there were three education ministries: the Ministry of Education, the Ministry of Higher Education, and the Ministry of Culture.[11] The State Council had the power to annul and revise inappropriate decisions made by them.

Another group that had an important say in the educational policies were the members of the Politburo and the Department of Propaganda of the Communist Party. Barnett alleges that they were the 'ultimate decision-making group within the ministry or other government agency in which they operated.'[12] While it is true that the party played an important role in the formulation of state policies, in our opinion, what accounted for their strength was the tremendous degree of overlap in the key personnel of the two organizations. For example, Lu Ting-i, the minister of culture, was also director of propaganda; and Chang Chi-ch'uan, director of the Office of Culture and Education, was also deputy director of the Propaganda Department.[13] Since our present purpose is to identify the decision-makers, the large amount of overlapping eliminates the problem of identifying the locus of power (in the state apparatus or the party).

The power of the decision-makers rested not only on their political control of the state apparatus and the party, but also on the support of the class whose interests they represented. The hegemonic ideology of this group was embodied in Marxism-Leninism and the thought of Mao Tse-tung. It defined the targets of development as the realization of 'socialist transformation of agriculture, handicraft industry, and capital industry and commerce, step by step throughout the country, and the task of realizing the socialist industrialization of the country'. The

Table 2 Party Membership of the Directors and Ministers of Education as Promulgated after Second NPC 1959

	Party Membership	First Known Date of Membership
Office of Culture and Education		
Director:		
Chang Chi-ch'un	CP (a)	BL (b)
Deputy Directors:		
Yang Hsiu-feng	CP	BL
Ch'ien Chun-jui	CP	BL
Chang Chia-fu	CP	BL
Fan Ch'ang-chiang	CP	— (c)
Hsu Mai-chin	CP	BL
Ministry of Culture		
Minister:		
Shen Yen-ping	CP	BL
Vice-ministers:		
Ch'ien Chun-jui	CP	BL
Hsia Yen	—	—
Hu Yu-chih	CP	—
Ch'en K'e-han	CP	BL
Lin Mo-han	CP	BL
Ministry of Education		
Minister:		
Yang Hsui-feng	CP	BL
Vice-ministers:		
Liu K'ai-feng	CP	BL
Tung Ch'un-tsai	CP	—
Yeh Sheng-t'ao	CP	BL
Liu Tzu-tsai	CP	—
Lin Li-ju	CP	BL

Source: Who's Who in Communist China (Hongkong: Union Research Institute, 1969) and Chinese Communist Who's Who (Taiwan: Institute of International Relations, 1976).
(a) CP: Member of the Communist Party.
(b) BL: Joined the CCP or involved in revolutional activities before 1949.
(c) —: Information not available.

Table 3 Party Membership of the Directors and Ministers of Education as Promulgated after Third NPC 1965

		Party Membership	First Known Date of Membership
Office of Culture and Education			
Director:	Chang Chi-ch'un	CP (a)	BL (b)
Deputy Directors:	Chang Chia-fu	CP	BL
	Hsu Mai-chin	CP	BL
	Kao Yun-p'ing	— (c)	—
	Chang Meng-hsu	—	—
Ministry of Culture			
Minister:	Lu Ting-i	CP	BL
Vice-ministers:	Hu Yu-chih	CP	BL
	Hsu Kuang-hsiao	—	—
	Hsu Ping-yu	CP	—
	Liu Pai-yu	—	—
	Shih Hsi-min	CP	BL
	Yen Chin-sheng	—	—
	Li Ch'i	CP	BL
	Lin Mo-han	CP	BL
	Hsia Wang-tung	CP	BL
	Chao Hsin-ch'u	—	—
Ministry of Higher Education			
Minister:	Chiang Nan-hsiang	CP	BL
Vice-ministers:	Liu Yang-chiao	—	—
	Kao Yi	—	—
	Tuan Lo-fu	—	—
	Huang Hsin-pai	—	—
Ministry of Education			
Minister:	Ho Wei	CP	BL
Vice-ministers:	Liu Chi-ping	CP	—
	Liu K'ai-feng	CP	BL
	Yeh Sheng-t'ao	CP	BL
	Lin Li-ju	CP	BL

Source: *Who's Who in Communist China* (Hongkong: Union Research Institute, 1969).

(a) CP: Member of the Communist Party.

(b) BL: Became a member of CCP or involved in revolutionary activities before liberation.

(c) —: Information not available.

aims of education were for national construction and movement towards socialism: 'Our educational policy must enable everyone who receives an education to develop morally, intellectually and physically and become a well-educated worker, imbued with socialist consciousness and culture.'[14] Educational policy, as embodied in the ideology of the policy-makers, was to benefit the whole population. Graduates from the educational system were not only to possess the necessary skills to partake in productive labour, but also to be actively supportive of the structure of the socialist system.

The majority of the members at the policy-making level belonged to the Communist Party. There was even a tendency to discriminate in favour of those who had joined the party before liberation, thus ensuring their commitment to the socialist ideology and helping to weed out any opportunists who only joined the party after its coming to power. All those who held the offices of director of education and culture, the minister of culture, the minister of education, and the minister of higher education during 1958–66 had joined the party before liberation, and of the twenty-seven vice-ministers and deputy directors, nineteen at least had joined the party or were involved in its activities before liberation.

This did not mean that the policy-makers were entirely free of capitalist ideology. It is only logical to assume that all the policy-makers in the fifties and sixties had been brought up during the feudal-capitalist period and exposed to its influences; however, overt evidence of bourgeois ideology or power lust among them is lacking. The struggles that arose within the hegemonic group usually appeared to be concerned with differing evaluations of objective conditions and the best strategies for development. The statements they made were couched in communist jargon and fitted acceptably within the framework of the hegemonic ideology, but because of the semantic similarity of the various articulations, it is all the more important to focus on the outcome of their policies, rather than their words, in seeking to identify their real goals—that is, which class benefited most from the policies they enunciated.

There were two main strategies of development posited before the Cultural Revolution. In discussing these two roads of development at this point, we shall single out only the two leading spokesmen, Mao Tse-tung and Liu Shao-ch'i. The two groups these individuals represented did not have the well-articulated factional structure characteristic of political groups in the West. Even studies analysing party history in terms of power struggle had to admit that 'these groups do not necessarily constitute "factions", if by factions we mean a self-conscious group bound together for a common purpose. The organization of these groups was on the whole rather diffuse.'[15] There was a great deal of fluidity in the composition of the groups involved. Individuals did not necessarily align themselves with one group or another throughout the period. Perhaps because of the particular nature of the communist ideology, with its emphasis on the common good and dynamics of interaction between a person's ideology and objective conditions, individual positions differed on different issues at different points of time. P'eng Te-huai, for example, was in favour of the policy of the Great Leap Forward (GLF) at its inception, but he later became its chief critic.

The adoption of any policy rested on the domination of a particular faction among the decision-makers. Power struggles, or at least political manoeuvring to procure the adoption of a set of policies, did occur. In 1959, P'eng Te-huai, the critic of the policy of the Great Leap Forward, was dismissed. This signified the triumph of its protagonists, Mao and his supporters. When the policy of the Great Leap Forward failed to bring forth the expected results, an attempt was made to review the case of P'eng in 1962, indicating that the opposition was gaining strength. The years preceding the Cultural Revolution were marked by a power struggle, characterized by political purges and the dismissal of key persons in the government, for example, Chou Yang and P'eng Chen. However, these shifting power alignments do not appear to have been a struggle for power alone, they appeared to be an integral part in the struggle for the adoption of certain strategies of development.

Judging from the public statements made by Liu Shao-ch'i and Mao Tse-tung, there would seem to have been no fundamental difference in the ultimate aims of these two leaders. Both agreed on the eventual movement of China towards socialism, and then communism. Both agreed that education was to serve proletarian interests and to be integrated with productive labour. However, they did differ in their interpretation of the role of social activ-

ism. (Mao allotted a more active role to man's social conscious- *# 1*
ness: 'While we recognize in general the development of history, *Mao*
the material determines the mental, and social being determines
social consciousness, we also—and indeed must—recognize the
reaction of mental on material things, of social consciousness on
social being and of the superstructure on the economic base.'[16] He
believed that mankind's social consciousness could be turned into
a force to change the world, and had faith in the activism of the
masses in transforming social reality. While Liu did not deny this *# 2*
possibility, he tended to place less importance on social activism *Liu*
and more on organization and the power of technology to trans- *Shao-ch'i*
form society. His writings in general deal more with self-discipline and party organization. In his own self-criticism during the
Cultural Revolution, he admitted that he distrusted the masses.) *!*
  Nonetheless, both men were flexible in their assessment of objective conditions. Mao asserted that a distinction should be made
between primary and secondary contradictions. Primary contradictions should be resolved first, and compromise could then be
made on secondary contradictions. Liu, using the same reasoning,
advocated a flexible approach in dealing with unresolved situations. In certain cases, he maintained, compromise not involving
principles could be made.[17]
  While both men were flexible in their approach to the analysis
of situations, their differing emphases on social activism often led
them to develop divergent perspectives of and strategies for educational development. Mao saw the more equal distribution of *more wants*
educational opportunities as the immediate task. He put more *approach*
emphasis than did Liu on ideology in the provision of education, *to educ.*
on raising the consciousness of the masses, assigning them a
more important role, and emphasizing both mass initiative and
effort. He was very critical of the stultifying effect of bureaucratization on mass initiative and was especially wary of the possible
emergence of a bureaucratic elite. Liu, on the other hand, attached *elitist*
greater importance to scientific and cultural education and was *approach*
less willing to compromise educational standards, the danger, as he *similar to*
saw it, of expansion or ideological education. He paid greater *capitalism*
attention to the limitations of objective conditions in the provision *education*
of education, placing more emphasis on the contribution of the
experts to educational development and the role of the organization in procuring a more efficient utilization of existing resources.

When the economy of China was growing, the question of re-source limitations could be avoided. The relative priorities given to expansion and consolidation and to ideological and scientific education were less crucial. But when crises came, the question of the relative priority of these alternatives came to a head and conflicts arose between the two leaders.

Of course, the ideologies of the two men did not remain static during the period under study. Changes in their position occurred with changing conditions. In 1958, Mao was very impatient with the rate of development in China; in 1959, with the change in objective conditions, he recognized that the process was more complicated than he had anticipated. The same dynamics can be identified in Liu's thought. In 1959, Liu allied with Mao to dismiss P'eng; but in 1962, he attempted to review the case. In the early fifties, both were apparently optimistic that the socialist era would soon usher in the end of antagonistic class conflict in soci-ety; in the sixties, their opinions diverged, with Liu adhering to his early optimism and Mao becoming more convinced than ever of the necessity for continuous class struggle.[18] Documents[19] re-leased since the Cultural Revolution trace the rift between them as far back as the late twenties, when they were fighting the War of Liberation. However, these documents have to be interpreted with caution, since they were released in a period of great politi-cal turmoil and with the explicit intention of justifying Liu's purge. Even if it is a fact that the two leaders disagreed in the late twenties, as these documents suggest, this does not preclude the possibility of their agreeing on occasion. Indeed, materials re-leased during the Cultural Revolution confirm that Liu initially supported Mao on the policies of the Great Leap Forward and disagreed with him on their viability only in the sixties.

It should not be assumed that these two individuals stood alone at the policy-making level and dominated its development. In-deed, no policy could be adopted without the support of other policy-makers and also the implementers. Judging from the kinds of policies these two advocated, Mao's preoccupation with ideo-logical education required a more radical restructuring of the educational system, hitting the very power base of the traditional elites. In advocating educational expansion, he sought to procure immediate benefits for the masses. It was quite natural that Mao's policy would gain most support from the proletariat who had been traditionally excluded from the educational system and stood to benefit from its expansion. However, the traditional elites stood to benefit more from Liu's policy of consolidating the educational system because, compared to the general populace, they were in a better position to take advantage of the limited educational facilities. During the period of Liu's ascendancy, his emphasis on scientific education strengthened the position of the traditional elites, who monopolized scientific knowledge even in the period of our analysis, and his reliance on the role of the bureaucracy in effecting social changes further increased the status of these elites and helped to ossify the existing power relations within the educational system. A more serious ramification of Liu's position was that these structures, which bore the imprints of the feudal-capitalist period, became hotbeds for the spawning of bourgeois values and practices. Through the educational activities carried on within the system, these values and practices were transmitted to the younger generation.[20] While the policies of Liu did not appear to be bourgeois in intent, in practice, they benefited mostly the bourgeois class, bolstering its position and recreating the bourgeois social formation in a socialist period. Liu was branded as a bourgeois renegade during the Cultural Revolution and is classified as 'bourgeois' in this analysis for these reasons, even though he appeared to be committed to communism in China.

IMPLEMENTATION LEVEL (GROUPS 3 AND 4)

At the local level, there were three administrative divisions: the provinces, autonomous regions, and the three municipalities of Peking, Shanghai, and Tientsin; special and autonomous districts and counties; towns and villages. Each of these divisions had its own People's Congress. Its executive, the People's Council, was responsible for the execution of law and drawing up of plans for local economic and cultural development, in accordance with the directives emanating from the centre. In each administrative division there were departments of education, responsible to both the educational departments at the next higher level and to the People's Congress. At the lowest level of the educational bureaucracy were the schools, which were responsible to the office of

Figure 4. Command Relationship of the Administration of Education

Administrative Divisions	Legislative Body	Executive Body	
National level	National People's Congress → → →	State Council → → →	Ministries of Education
	↓	↓	↓
Provincial level	People's Congress → → → → → → →	People's Council → → →	Departments of Education
	↓	↓	↓
County level	People's Congress → → → → → → →	People's Council → → →	Departments of Education
	↓	↓	↓
Village & town	People's Congress → → → → → → →	People's Council → → →	Departments of Education

* The arrow shows the direction of command.

education nearest to them. The universities were responsible directly to the minister of education.[21]

While the policies were drafted by the centre, implementers (teachers and cadres) still had leeway for individual action. The location of new schools, the curricula within the schools, and the appointment of teachers were under local jurisdiction. Within the confines of the classroom, teachers had considerable freedom in the organization of teaching activities and the grading of students.

The majority of the implementers were of the bourgeois background who used to monopolize the educational system before liberation. The percentage of staff drawn from the landlord or bourgeois class might decrease lower down the educational ladder. At the university level there were few from working class origins. It was reported in 1958 that 2,474 professors and assistant professors of forty-six institutions of higher learning came from landlord or bourgeois class origins.[22] There was not only a physical carryover of educators from the nationalist period; there was also a carryover of their ideology or work style. Rectification campaigns had been carried out in the early fifties to eliminate bourgeois thought, but remnants of bourgeois ideology remained. As late as 1967, Mao remarked: 'Although the social and economic systems have changed, yet the vestiges of reactionary ideas left behind from the old era are still found in the minds of quite sizable a section of people. This means ideas of the bourgeoisie ... will not change overnight. The change will take time — a very long time. This is the class struggle in society.'[23] As a result, the educational system at the implementation level remained a bastion of the traditional elites who had been ousted from political power. With changing economic conditions, their power no longer resided in their dominant position in the political and economic spheres; now it resided in their monopoly on technical skills. The continuance of their privileged existence rested on their continued monopoly of technology and on the importance placed on technology in the educational system.

The traditional elites did not oppose the expansion of education outright. However, they objected to the expansion of educational opportunities at the expense of academic standards. They denigrated the work-study schools that were supported by Mao in his efforts to extend educational opportunities. Preferring an

work-study schools

academic educational system with fine buildings and modern equipment, they were unwilling to reorganize the academic curricula to serve proletarian ideals. To their minds, the educated person had a higher status than the labourer. They curtailed the time given to productive labour once pressure from the centre was released in the 1960s. Influenced by the Confucian concept of education, they continued to encourage rote learning and reduced ideological education to the memorization of Marxist-Leninist texts and party directives.

These attitudes represented a holdover of the traditional concept of the function of education, that is, to produce scholar-gentlemen who stood above the masses, and to impart to them theoretical knowledge which stood above politics and was divorced from practice. The class bias in their ideology is apparent. By emphasizing high academic standards, the position and prestige of those who already possessed good academic qualifications were bolstered. By inculcating the same values into the younger generation, the conditions supportive of the traditional elite's existence could be perpetuated. By raising educational standards at the expense of educational expansion, the traditional elites could effectively limit the provision of education to the masses and ensure the monopoly of education for themselves and their posterity.

Given the political situation in China, they could not blatantly try to consolidate their position, but Liu's developmental strategies of capitalizing and relying on the expertise of the traditional elites tended to work to their advantage. His reliance on these technocrats opened up for them an avenue to power. Just as the opposition party in Miliband's analysis of the capitalist formation had to compromise with the existing structure, so these bourgeois elements had to compromise with socialism to ensure their own continued existence. Liu's policy of socialist development towards communism offered them a better alternative than did Mao's. But there is a distinction between Liu's bourgeois line at the policy-making level and that at the implementation level. The Liuist line was purported to develop a socialist educational system, though in effect it benefited the bourgeois class. At the implementation level, the bourgeois element simply preferred the traditional capitalist system of education because its preservation would inadvertently preserve their interest.

Though the majority of the implementers might come from a bourgeois background, not all were opposed to communism or the Maoist strategy of development. If that had been the case, the communists would not have come to power in the first place. Some among them actively criticized their traditionally oriented colleagues for their reluctance to change. During the Great Leap Forward, for example, one party secretary criticized teachers for failing to institute radical reform in the curricula and for treating the traditional curricula as sacred. Nonetheless, support for Mao's strategies of development was in the minority in the late fifties. Even some of the peasants opposed the work-study schools and students remained relatively passive. This is understandable: for centuries, the Chinese have revered the scholar and deferred to the judgment of intellectuals. In the sixties, however, with the growing evidence of the advantages of the work-study schools, the ossification of the elites, and the cumulative effects of political campaigns, the students and the proletariat became more active. Sympathy swung in favour of Mao. By the mid-sixties, it was the dissatisfaction of the students and the proletariat (especially the peasants among them) with the existing educational system and their involvement in the struggle that turned the tables in Mao's favour and sparked off the Cultural Revolution.

At the local level, support swung to Mao's line of development for various reasons. Some were genuinely sympathetic to his socialist principles. Others favoured his strategies because they wanted a more equal distribution of educational opportunities. Rural cadres and peasants welcomed the schools being brought to their doorstep and geared to their needs. Still others gave their support out of a growing awareness that Liu's policies might lead to the entrenchment of a new elite and the strengthening of capitalist tendencies. Students were critical of the esoteric nature of curricula that were divorced from reality.

Because of the important role eventually played by the proletariat and the students in the balance of power at the local level and the emphasis placed on mass mobilization in the hegemonic ideology, the demands of the clientele of the educational system, that is, the proletariat and the students, could not be ignored. They must therefore be considered alongside the cadres as one of the components that made up the social groups at the implementation level.

Table 4 Social Groups in Chinese Educational System

	Proletarian Ideology	Bourgeois Ideology
Policy-making Level	1. Mao and supporters at the central level	2. Liu and supporters at the central level
Implementation Level	3. Cadres, teachers, and students	4. Cadres, teachers, and students

The presence of these different groups resulted in power struggles at the implementation level to decide on the manner in which the policies were to be carried out. The manner of implementation determined to a large extent the success or failure of the policies which in turn shaped future decisions made at the centre. The policies formulated at the centre were affected by their own internal power politics as well as by the alignments of power at the implementation level, the decisions made there, the manner in which they were carried out, and their outcomes. The course of educational development was very much the result of the interplay of these contradictions and struggles at both the policy-making and the implementation levels.

Hegemonic Ideology:
Educational Thoughts
of Mao Tse-tung

While Marxism-Leninism is the basis of the hegemonic ideology in China, its policies have been guided by the more practically oriented thoughts of Mao Tse-tung. Even though Mao did not have full control of China at all times—he resigned from his position as chairman of the People's Republic in 1959 and did not stage a comeback until the socialist education campaign in 1963— he retained his position as chairman of the party, and his thoughts remained the guidelines of the policies formulated. Even when policies actually ran counter to Mao's precepts, they were still invoked as justification for the direction taken. As he himself pointed out during the Cultural Revolution, he was treated like 'an old man at his funeral'.[1]

ORIGINS OF MAO TSE-TUNG'S THOUGHTS

The thoughts of Mao Tse-tung were tremendously consistent throughout his life. Even before he became a Marxist, he was very critical of existing educational practices. Ever since the summer of 1920, he had considered himself 'in theory and to some extent in action a Marxist'. True, there were variations in Mao's views on education during the Kiangsi-Soviet period (1928–34), the Civil War (1935–49), and after the establishment of the People's Republic in 1949,[2] but throughout these times, he remained Marxist in principle.

To Marx, Mao owed the guiding principles behind his thoughts, the chief of which was the idea of dialectical materialism, which he expressed in his own writings, 'On Contradiction' and 'On Practice'. He subscribed to Marx's view that 'the economy is the real foundation on which rise legal and political superstructures, and to which correspond definite forms of social consciousness'.[3] Change is seen as a process in which contradictory elements of a social phenomenon are in conflict. During the process, one aspect prevails, eliminating the other. As the old contradiction is eliminated, new ones arise. As a result, matter evolves from level to level and new characteristics emerge.

To Lenin, Mao owed the more practical aspects of his educational theories, especially those in the area of statecraft and educational administration. Lenin held that political consciousness did not manifest itself spontaneously among the proletariat; it had to be instilled by the elite or vanguard. He gave very great importance to the role of the party in state administration. To prevent the overcentralized control of the party, Lenin advocated democratic centralism: dependence on the coordination of the party and on the will of the people. The influences of these two aspects of Lenin's thoughts can be detected in Mao's 'On the People's Democratic Dictatorship' and in his 'Some Questions Concerning Methods of Leadership'.

Although the thoughts of Mao Tse-tung were based essentially on Marxism-Leninism, they had some distinct characteristics of their own, in that he integrated the principles of Marxism into the Chinese milieu. Instead of focusing on the class consciousness of the workers in starting a revolution, he depended on the peasants. Mao also trusted the masses in shaping their own fate to a far greater extent than did Lenin.

The influences of the Chinese background on Mao's thoughts have been dealt with in detail by Ch'en.[4] Mao assumed that the masses were, in the main, not only poor but unspoiled by sophistication. He believed in the malleability of man's nature through education and persuasion, including the use of criticism and self-criticism. These characteristics, Ch'en holds, bear strong resemblances to the philosophies of such men as Mencius and Wang Fu-chih. Ch'en also maintains that Mao's philosophy shows characteristics that derive from his provincial upbringing—his pragmatism, his emphasis on investigation and reason, his concern with the relationship between knowledge and action, reform and revolution, and his pride in the Chinese race.

Perhaps the definitive influence on Mao's philosophical development was his years of revolutionary experience and especially the educational experiments of the Yenan Period[5] which became the prototype of many such later experiments. It was a time when the communists were on the defensive, resisting the constant attacks of the KMT in the 1930s. The educational experiments of this period were innovative and flexible: the curricula were reduced to the basics, the local population became involved, and learning activities were organized whenever and wherever *Cuba* possible outside the confines of the conventional classrooms. This experience in educational construction convinced Mao that the western system of education with its well-equipped school buildings was ill suited to the reality of Chinese society, as was the traditional Chinese educational system with its preoccupation with academic pursuit to meet the needs of the day. He held the belief that it was necessary to develop an alternative model which was 'national, scientific, and popular'. He was further convinced of the primary importance of changing the consciousness of the masses as well as actively involving them in the developmental process. *changing through words + action both*

It is difficult to separate the sources of the different aspects of Mao's thoughts on education—whether they arose from Marxism, Leninism, or his Chinese background. For example, his belief in the malleability of the masses might have arisen from the thoughts of Mencius, from Rousseau, or from both, for he had been exposed to both thinkers. Likewise, it is difficult to say whether his emphasis on practice resulted mainly from his Hunanese origin, his revolutionary experiences, or the dialectical materialism of Marx. Whatever the case, it is important to recognize that Mao did not adopt Marxism unquestioningly; he adapted it and integrated it with his Chinese experience.

THE ROLE OF EDUCATION IN SOCIETY

According to Mao, the educational system is part of the cultural network of a country. He accepted the basic Marxist principle that education is part of the superstructure of society and economy the infrastructure: 'Any given culture [as an ideological form] is a reflection of the politics and economics of a given society, and the former in turn has a tremendous influence and effect upon the latter. Economics is the base and politics the concentrated expression of economics. This is the fundamental view of the relations of culture to politics and economics.'[6] Further, he believed that education is a propaganda tool of the ruling class and serves its interests alone. He had solid grounds for his belief. In feudal China, 90 percent of the population were peasants, but education was controlled by the landlords, and the ideology within the educational system represented that of the landlord class. In a socialist society, Mao held, education should be turned to serve the interests of the workers and peasants. Mao denied that education or culture could be above politics: 'In the world, all culture, all literature and art, belongs to definite classes and is geared to definite political lines. There is, in fact, no such thing as art for art's sake, art that stands above classes or that which is detached from or independent of politics.'[7]

The first signs of Mao's recognition of the reciprocal role of education and economy, of the need for the continued growth and development of education to ensure a strong economic base, and of education as an investment in economic construction, appeared during the Kiangsi-Soviet period. Mao put great emphasis on the role of education in creating an outlook necessary for the development of a socialist economy. Through education, the younger generation would acquire a love of labour and an understanding of the proletarian ideals and ideology.

What were the aims of education? The educational system was to create individuals that were both 'red and expert'. 'Redness' refers to the possession of the communist outlook. It was the duty of the educational system to instil into the young political awareness: 'We must strengthen our ideological and political work. Both students and intellectuals should study hard ... they must make progress both ideologically and politically which means they should study Marxism, current events and political problems. Not to have a correct political viewpoint is like having no soul.'[8] Mao was also critical of the exclusive pursuit of academic learning; expertise should include the mastery of theoretical knowledge as well as the practical and technical proficiency of that specialty. To him, 'redness' and expertise were inextricably linked; their relationship stood for 'the unity of two opposites. It is certainly necessary to criticize and repudiate the tendency to ignore politics. It is necessary to oppose the politician on the one hand and the practicalist who has gone astray on the other.'[9]

While Mao's basic educational philosophy changed little throughout his life, his priorities did, accommodating to changing objective conditions. In his report to the Central Executive Committee in 1934 he wrote:

> What is the general line of our Soviet culture and education? Our general line is to educate in the communist spirit the broad masses of labouring people, to use culture and education to serve revolutionary war and class struggle, to unite education with labour, to make it possible for the broad masses of the Chinese people to enjoy culture and happiness. What is the central task of our Soviet cultural reconstruction? Our central task is to introduce compulsory education for all our people, to launch large scale socialist education, vigorously to eliminate illiteracy and to create a large number of high level cadres to lead the revolutionary struggle.[10]

In the later thirties, during the period of Japanese aggression, he took a more militant stand. In 1937, he noted that the central purpose of educational policy was to 'institute education for national defence, radically reform the existing educational policy and system. All projects that are not urgent and all measures that are not rational must be discarded. Newspapers, books, and magazines, films, plays, literature, and art should all serve national defence.'[11] Later, in 1940, he realized that 'national defence education' was no longer adequate. He wrote that the central task of Chinese revolution was still mainly that of combating 'foreign imperialism', but to it he added 'domestic feudalism'. The new democratic culture was to be 'nationalistic, scientific, and of the masses'.

After the establishment of the republic, he saw the aim of education as socialist construction. His emphasis shifted from nationalism to socialism: 'Our educational policy must enable everyone who receives an education to develop morally, intellectually, and physically and become a well educated worker imbued with socialist consciousness.'[12] Education was henceforth to serve proletarian ideals and should be integrated with productive labour. In the mid-sixties, after twenty years of continuous efforts, the tremendous difficulties in ideological transformation became apparent. In 1967, Mao openly remarked that despite changes in the social and economic systems, the reactionary ideas of the previous era remained. Bourgeois ideology was still deeply rooted in a large section of the population, and attempts to eradicate these ideas, inherent in the class struggle of every society, would 'take time, and a very long time'.[13] This recognition of the difficulties involved and the time it would take to bring about real ideological changes led Mao to increase his emphasis on raising social consciousness and to renew efforts in that direction both during and after the Cultural Revolution.

MAO'S VIEW OF KNOWLEDGE

good question

Where does knowledge come from? According to Mao, it comes from social practice: the struggle for production and class struggle. Through the act of production, man becomes aware of his relation to nature, to other men, and to himself. His knowledge is influenced by class struggle, by his political relationships, and experiences—in short, by his entire social milieu. It is this composite social being that determines his thinking. 'Ever since class society came into being, the world has had only two kinds of knowledge: knowledge of the struggle for production and knowledge of class struggle. Natural science and social science are the crystallization of these two kinds of knowledge, and philosophy is the generalization and summation of nature and the knowledge of society.'[14]

While recognizing the determining influence of the environment on man's consciousness, Mao was also aware of the effect of social consciousness on social being: 'While we recognize in general the development of history, the material determines the mental, and social being determines social consciousness. We also—and indeed, must—recognize the reaction of mental on material things, of social consciousness on social being and of the superstructure on the economic base.'[15] Once knowledge has been grasped, these ideas turn into material forces that can change society, and indeed, the world. The only test to see if knowledge is correct is to put it into practice. That is why the concept of practice figures so prominently in Mao's educational thought.

very true

one reason why capitalist education can never work for the masses — its too separated from real life

The first stage in the acquisition of knowledge is the perceptual stage of cognition. During this stage, man receives separate and isolated sensory impressions. Through repeated exposure, these sensory impressions are received many times. A cognitive leap then occurs, and at the second stage, man forms concepts. He grasps the essence, the totality, and the internal relation of things. This is the stage of rational knowledge. The progression from perception to cognition represents a leap from quantitative to qualitative thought. However, knowledge gained through perception and ratiocination is incomplete unless one applies it to one's environment: 'If you want to know a certain thing or a certain class of things, you must personally participate in the practical struggle to change reality, to change that thing or class of things ... only through personal participation in the practical struggle to change reality can you uncover the essence of that thing or class of things and comprehend them.'[16] Knowledge arises through practice (class struggle and the struggle for production). In turn, practice is the test of the correctness of knowledge. Through practice, man makes more observations and the cycle is repeated. Inherent in this dialectical view of knowledge is the implication that knowledge is not absolute and dogmatism is to be avoided.

Because of the important role Mao assigned to practice in the acquisition of knowledge, practice is considered an integral part of the educational curricula in revolutionary China. The unity of theory and practice is constantly emphasized by the hegemonic group. Students were to take part in productive labour in order to put the theories learnt in the classroom into practice. They were also to take part in class struggle—to integrate with the workers and acquire the proletarian outlook.

CURRICULUM

Mao was critical of the educational curriculum both before and after the communists came into power. In 1917, when he was still a student in the First Normal School, he described the curriculum in this way: 'In the educational system of our country, required courses are as thick as hairs on a cow. ... Speculating on the intentions of the educators, one is led to wonder if they did not design such an unwieldy curriculum in order to exhaust the students, to trample their bodies, and ruin their lives.'[17] In 1965, he levelled the same criticism at the curriculum: 'From entering primary school to leaving college is altogether sixteen or seventeen years. I feel that for over twenty years people will not see rice, mustard, wheat, or millet growing; nor will they see how workers work, nor how peasants till the fields, nor how people do business. Moreover, their health will be ruined.'[18] He suggested that the years of education should be cut short, the curriculum trimmed of unnecessary courses, and the remaining courses simplified.

In addition, he was dissatisfied with the content of school texts. He accepted the usefulness of traditional academic expertise; however, he pointed out that the content of many of these courses was divorced from reality: 'Teachers of philosophy do not guide students to study the logic of the Chinese revolution; teachers of economics do not guide them to study the characteristics of the Chinese economy; teachers of political science do not guide them to study the tactics of the Chinese revolution; teachers of military science do not guide them to study the strategy and tactics adapted to China's special features.'[19] In the same article, 'Reform our Study', he denounced research workers who confined their interests to the study of 'empty' theories. He criticized those who did practical work without considering objective conditions. He also noted an urban bias in the textbooks used in the rural primary schools. The materials did not have any practical value for the peasants and tended to turn them against education. This problem was closely related to who controlled the curriculum. Mao felt that it was usually drafted by the government department without reference to local needs. Even in those areas under communist control, peasants lacked the power to change the curriculum when it did not meet their needs; their only recourse was to boycott the schools. Mao suggested that people would take a more active interest if they were involved in the formulation of the local curriculum and were able to accommodate it to their desires and needs. Instructional materials should also reflect local characteristics. Texts on agriculture should be compiled. More local and indigenous resources should be used. Literature should draw examples from everyday life. The same applied to natural science; everyday examples should be used.

Mao was especially critical of the lack of practical work within the curricula. In 1940, he wrote:

Now let us take a look at certain students, those brought up in schools that are completely cut off from the practical activities of society. What about them? A person goes from a primary school of this kind all the way through to a university of the same kind, graduates, and is reckoned to have a stock of learning. He has not taken part in any practical activities or applied what he has learnt to any field of life. Can such a person be regarded as a completely developed intellectual. Hardly so ... in my opinion, because his knowledge is still incomplete.[20]

In order to expose these 'incomplete' intellectuals to reality, Mao recommended that they work in the countryside for a few years to learn about agriculture, botany, fertilizers, and soil and water conservation, and to integrate with the proletariat. Alternatively, for the cities, he recommended that schools be attached to the factories, so that the students could learn a variety of practical technical skills. It was only through practical experience that students could become intellectuals in the true sense of the word.

Mao has written little on the content of the curriculum, that is, on what subjects should be included besides the basic skills of reading, writing, and mathematics. However, he rejected neither western science nor the Chinese heritage. In 1938, in an article on what Chinese Communist Party members should study, he encouraged them to study both China's history, which goes back many thousands of years, and contemporary conditions. Only though reviewing history from Confucius to Sun Yat-sen could one encompass the valuable legacy and guide the revolutionary movement. At the same time, he emphasized learning from the experience of foreign countries:

We should assimilate whatever is useful to use today, not only from the earlier cultures of other nations, for example, from the culture of the various capitalist countries in the Age of Enlightenment. However, we should not gulp down any of this foreign material uncritically, but must treat it as we do our food—first chewing it, then submitting it to the workings of the stomach and intestines with their juices and secretions, and separating it into nutrients to be absorbed and waste matter to be discarded—before it can nourish us. To advocate 'wholesale westernization' is wrong.[21]

The same warning went for the study of China's past: 'It is imperative to separate the fine old culture of the people, which had a more or less democratic and revolutionary character, from all the decadence of the old feudal ruling class.'[22] His purpose in recommending the study of China's past and that of foreign countries was to give these studies 'a proper place as a science, respecting their dialectical development'. Such studies were to guide students to look forward and not backward.

Mao saw the inculcation of socialist ideology as an essential part of the curriculum. If due importance were not given to ideological work, economic and technical work would go astray. As early as 1939, he remarked: 'All work in school is for the purpose of transforming the students ideologically. Political education is the central link, and it is undesirable to have too many subjects. Class education, party education, and work must be strengthened.'[23] Marxism was more than just a part of the substantive content of the curriculum, however. As Mao wrote in 1941, Marxism-Leninism was not the target, but the arrow. It provided the methods to approach and interpret a problem. One was to use the theory and methods of dialectical materialism to make a systematic and thorough investigation of the environment and to solve the problems thus identified.

The thoughts of Marx were to intertwine with all subject matter. When Mao taught the Chinese characters for 'hands' and 'feet' to the peasants in 1925, he pointed out that while hands and feet created wealth, the peasants and workers who created the wealth did not receive it.[24] The same rationale lay behind his emphasis on productive work. Its function was to integrate the intellectuals with the workers, to make the intellectuals understand and communicate with the working class, and identify with them.

TEACHING METHODS

In the previous section, we looked at certain guidelines proposed by Mao in drafting the curriculum, which was to be short, precise, relevant, practical, and to have a correct ideological approach. After using these guidelines, how was the teacher to present his lesson?

Mao objected to the traditional Chinese view that the teacher imparts immutable and eternal truths to his students. He recognized that knowledge is relative and learning is an ongoing process. Teachers should also learn from their students.

Our writers and artists, scientists and technicians, professors and teachers, are all educating students, educating the people. Being educators and teachers, they themselves must first be educated. ... We have to learn while teaching, and be pupils while serving as teachers. To be a good teacher, one must first be a good pupil. There are many things which cannot be learnt from books alone; one must learn from those engaged in production, from the workers, from the poor and lower middle peasants, and, in schools, from the students, from those one teaches.[25]

Mao deplored the public school system of the early twentieth century, in which teachers were remote from their students and neither had any affection for the other, in which teachers cherished only money and students only the diploma that could be traded for money. In this respect, he thought traditional Chinese educational methods were superior to the more modern ones in that the pupils were much closer to the teacher, and the teacher, to a greater degree, understood the needs and abilities of his students.

He was far from authoritarian in his perception of the student-teacher relationship. He encouraged students to 'dare to think, dare to speak and dare to act'. He advised educators in 1964 that: 'There are teachers who ramble on and on when they lecture; they should let their students doze off. If your lecture is no good, why insist on others listening to you? Rather than keeping your eyes open and listening to boring lectures, it is better to get some refreshing sleep. You don't have to listen to nonsense, you can rest your brain instead.'[26]

In the organization of lessons at the university level, he urged professors to have their lecture notes printed and distributed before class to allow more time for discussion and further clarification. He saw the teacher more as an organizer who prepares materials on a given subject and allows the students to learn at their own pace.

He believed, moreover, that teachers should understand the language of their pupils. He criticized the use of long and complicated turns of phrase and rhetoric, and advocated a concise and clear style. The chapters Mao himself prepared were written simply, employing uncomplicated sentence structure, a limited vocabulary, and concisely organized data.[27]

With regard to teaching methods, he offered ten precepts for teachers:

(1) resort to the method of enlightenment [abolish inculcation];

(2) from the short range to the long range;

(3) from the superficial to the deep;

(4) speak in the popular language;

(5) be explicit;

(6) make what you say interesting;

(7) aid speech with gesticulation;

(8) review the concepts taught last time;

(9) there must be an outline;

(10) the method of discussion must be adopted.[28]

These points may appear to us to be simply common-sense and general, but they show Mao's clear understanding of what went on in the Chinese classroom and the common pitfalls of the teachers. The points he brought forth are qualities one always looks for in a teacher.

As early as 1964, Mao criticized the examination and the grading system. 'Our present method of conducting examinations is a method for dealing with the enemy, not a method for dealing with the people. It is a method of surprise attack, asking oblique or strange questions. This is still the same method as the old eight-legged essay. I do not approve of this.'[29] During the Cultural Revolution, a wholesale transformation took place. The examination system described above was replaced by open-book and take-home examinations at the secondary and university levels. Examinations became an opportunity whereby students could review what they did not know and look for solutions. As for grading the students' performance, Mao attached great importance to creativity and originality: 'For instance, if one sets twenty questions and some students answer half of them and answer them well, and some of the answers are very good and contain creative ideas, then one can give them 100 percent. If some other students answer all twenty questions and answer them correctly, but answer them simply by reciting from their textbooks and lectures, without any creative ideas, they should be given 50 to 60 percent.'[30]

ADMINISTRATION

Mao adopted Lenin's idea of democratic centralism in the administration of education, but he put a stronger reliance on the participation of the masses. As early as the Yenan Period, he was critical of the strict control government had on education: 'We only know how to have government come in and operate the schools. We do not understand how to apply correctly the force of the masses, how to have schools run by the people themselves, in accord with their own ambitions; therefore, both the form and content of education is to be decided by the people ... we must take the majority of or perhaps all the primary schools and turn them over to the masses to run by themselves.'[31]

Central government, in his view, should concentrate on planning and should not interfere unless problems arose. In most cases, official intervention in education should occur only when giving guidance on matters of policy or supplying necessary material aid. He asserted that: 'The policy of popular management cannot be divorced from that of government assistance. Popular management of schools cannot be allowed to run its own course. It is incorrect to think that we will lighten our responsibilities through popular management; in fact the reverse is true, we must strengthen our leadership.'[32] He perceived the devolution of authority, not as an opting out of responsibilities by the central government, but as an opportunity to involve people at the local level.

His concern with putting the control of education in the hands of the people directly involved extended to night schools, literacy classes, the Communist Party, the communist army, the youth league, and all the government departments that were engaged in ideological and political work. However, we shall here focus on the organization of the regular schools.

The vehicle for school management and administration was the 'leading group'. In 1943, Mao pointed out that 'a school of a hundred people certainly cannot run well if it does not have a leading group of several people, or a dozen or more, which is formed in accordance with the actual circumstances (and not thrown together artificially) and is composed of the most active, upright, and alert of the teachers, the other staff, and the students.'[33] He held that this group of leaders should include as many elements as possible: students, teachers, workers, peasants, parents, and other interested individuals. Those selected should be chosen for their devotion to the cause of socialism, their good relations with the people in the community, their ability to innovate, to act independently, and to practise self-discipline. Mao expected them to keep in close contact with the people they represented and to develop the ability to translate the people's desires into specific policies which the community concerned would accept.

These local administrative leaders were to have real power. They would run schools according to local needs and have genuine authority in such areas as the hiring of teachers, the determination of salaries and class size, the selection of school sites, the formulation of the curricula, and the compilation of texts.

In administering these schools, the local leaders or cadres were to rely on the people. Mao told a visiting Nepalese delegation in 1964 that 'strength comes from the masses. Without reflecting the demands of the masses, nobody is equal to his job. One should gain knowledge from the masses, lay down the policy, and then go back to educate the masses.'[34] The cadres were supposed to investigate local conditions and discuss problems with those concerned before making decisions affecting the administration of the schools. Mao put great reliance on fact-finding meetings: 'Holding fact-finding meetings is the simplest, most practical, and most reliable method from which I have derived much benefit. It is a better school than any university.'[35] As far back as the early 1940s, Mao had advocated that all issues be discussed openly, so that the public would be involved at all levels. The local leaders, in turn, were to listen to all ideas, even those that opposed the official line, and they were admonished to show humility and avoid arrogance.

Information gathered from the fact-finding meetings and the larger mass meetings was to be shared among the different committees and departments. The role of the leaders was to collect the unsystematic and scattered ideas, organize them, interpret them, and implement the policies decided on. This was Mao's idea of the mass line; all the ideas were to arise from the masses and ultimately be fed back to them.

These remained the guidelines of educational development throughout the period under study. Differences of opinion sometimes occurred on the interpretation of Mao's thoughts or the strategies to be adopted in pursuit of his principles. This was one of the sources of conflict that subsequently arose in the process of educational development in China. Conflict notwithstanding, the opposing strategies that were proposed and implemented referred to the thoughts of Mao as their justification. The thoughts of Mao were the embodiment of the hegemonic ideology that provided the guidelines for educational development in China during the fifties and sixties.

★4★

Economic Development: 1949–1957

The hegemonic ideology provides the guidelines of educational development but it is not the only important determinant. Objective conditions play an equally important role. In this chapter, we shall look at the economic conditions that decision-makers and implementers faced on the eve of the Great Leap Forward in 1958.

PROPERTY RELATIONS OF PRODUCTION

One major economic distinction between pre-liberation and post-liberation Chinese society is the different form of ownership. Another is the distribution of wealth. The dominant mode of property ownership after liberation was state ownership. By 1953, about 3,000 foreign-owned enterprises had been confiscated without compensation. These included many of the major capital-intensive industries, particularly mining, smelting, iron works, communications, transport, and some consumer industries. Taken together, these accounted for 26 percent of the gross national industrial product.[1]

The takeover of private enterprises owned by nationals was accomplished in several stages. Initially only the supply of raw materials and major consumer goods, and the sale of finished products, came under state control. In the second stage, the surviving private enterprises signed contracts with the government in which production targets were specified; after fulfilling the state quota, they could still manufacture their own goods for private sale. Then, in 1952, the state entered actively into the management of these enterprises as well, and shared in their profits. Many of the owners remained as managers, working alongside personnel representing the state. This transformation of private

Table 5 Socialist Transformation of Private Industry 1953–56

Year	State Enterprise (percent)	Joint State-Private Enterprise (percent)	Private Enterprise Executing Orders for Goods (percent)	Private Industry (percent)
1953	57.5	5.7	22.8	14.0
1954	62.8	12.3	19.6	5.3
1955	67.7	16.1	13.2	3.0
1956	67.5	32.5	—	—

Source: *Ten Great Years* (Peking: Foreign Languages Press, 1960), p. 38.

enterprise into joint state-private enterprise was at first carried out piecemeal. Later, whole trades and branches of industries were transferred from private to joint ownership, locality by locality. By the end of 1956, enterprises with capital totalling more than 2,000 million yuan (about $1,200 million U.S.) had become state-private enterprises. Wholly state-owned enterprises accounted for 67.5 percent of the total industrial output, state-private enterprises for 32.5 percent, and private enterprises virtually disappeared.[2]

Workers did not own their means of production directly. Their ownership was mediated through the state. Neither did they share completely in the fruits of their labour. The bourgeoisie continued to share in the surplus value. Before 1956, they retained 25 percent of the profit from enterprises in which they had an investment. After February 1956, this was reduced to a fixed interest of about 5 percent per annum on any private assets they had invested.[3] The rest of the gross output went in state taxes, which were re-invested in state industries and in salary and welfare premiums for the workers. Gurley estimated that state re-investment was 25 percent which, to a certain extent, accounted for the tremendous rate of industrial growth during this period.[4]

After liberation, workers were paid according to their work, skill, and experience, but not yet according to their needs. The salaries of the former managerial and technical staff were maintained, but new recruits to these top positions were paid considerably less. The top incomes were commonly reported to be forty or fifty times as large as the lowest income but the differential between the new recruits and the workers was only about 3.5 times. In 1955, there was a major restructuring of the wage scales to make them more 'rational'. With this move came a growing trend to substitute wage payment with piece rates. By 1956, about 42 percent of the workers were paid on this basis and the income differential between managerial or technical staff and workers in some factories increased to 7:1.[5]

In the early fifties, Chinese workers made substantial advances in their quality of life. The average annual wage of the workers and managerial staff increased from 350 yuan (about $58 U.S.) in 1949 to 694 yuan (about $116 U.S.) in 1957.[6] In addition, there were also provisions for income security, supplementary benefits in health, welfare, housing, daycare, and other benefits by either the state or the enterprise for which they worked.

In agriculture, about 700 million mou (about 110 million acres) of privately owned land and also the means of production (draught animals, ploughs, etc.) were confiscated and distributed among 300 million poor and landless peasants, for an average of about 11 mou (about 1.7 acres) per household. Peasants now retained the annual dues of 70,000 catties (about 92,000 million pounds) of grain they had formerly given to the landlords.[7]

Land redistribution had gone on for a number of years. It dated back to the thirties in some districts that had come under communist rule before national liberation; in others, redistribution only occurred after 1949. In some districts, the process was relatively peaceful; in others, it was accompanied by much violence. It has been vividly described in Hinton's Fanshen and Yang's The Chinese Family in the Communist Revolution.[8] As a result of land redistribution, the percentage of poor peasants dropped from 60 percent to 30 percent in the early fifties.[9] This equality of land ownership was not absolute; former landlords retained the land they could work on their own, and this generally included the better land and equipment. Ownership of land was still private and the households remained the primary units of production.

The formation of mutual aid teams (about eight to ten households working together) began with the peasants pooling their

**Table 6 Per Household Holdings of Land,
Draught Animals, Plows, and Water Wheels 1954**

	Land (in mou)	Draught Animals (per head)	Plows (unit)	Water Wheels (unit)
Average	15.25	0.64	0.54	0.10
Poor Peasants	12.46	0.47	0.41	0.07
Middle Peasants	19.01	0.91	0.74	0.13
Rich Peasants	25.09	1.15	0.87	0.22
Landlords	12.16	0.23	0.23	0.04
Others	7.05	—	—	—

Source: John Wong, 'Mutual Aid Cooperation in China's Agricultural Collectivization', *The China Mainland Review*
(June 1967), p. 384.

labour, farm implements, and animals. At first, this was done on a
seasonal basis. The teams were usually dissolved at the end of
the planting or harvesting seasons. Later on, they were organized on a permanent basis. The distribution of profits in these
mutual aid teams was made according to the amount of labour
the peasants spent on production and their contribution of land
and draught animals. By 1954, there were about 10 million
mutual aid teams comprising about 58 percent of the peasant
households, about half of them seasonal, and the other half on a
regular basis.[10] In the mid-fifties, these mutual aid teams were
superseded by agricultural cooperatives; some of these were
formed as early as 1950, others in the second half of 1955. These
early cooperatives consisted of about thirty to forty households,
each of which owned its own land. Distribution of profits continued to be made according to labour and their contribution of
land, implements, and animals. Gradually, these early cooperatives evolved into a more advanced form in which the land and
other capital goods were held on a collective basis. Earnings were
distributed only on the basis of the work done. By 1956, about 96
percent of the peasant households belonged to cooperatives; of
these 668,000 were of the more advanced type and 84,000 of the
earlier type.[11]

FORCES OF PRODUCTION

Before liberation in 1949, the level of mechanization of China's industries was low; the technologically advanced capital-intensive industries were mainly foreign-owned and concentrated on the extraction of non-renewable resources. In the first two years following liberation, the state directed its efforts to fighting inflation. By the time monetary and fiscal stability was restored in 1952, the government was committed to a Soviet model of development which concentrated mostly on capital-intensive development, especially in heavy industry. According to the First Five Year Plan (FFYP), 694 above-norm projects (that is, industries equipped with the most up-to-date techniques) and 23,000 below-norm projects were to be constructed. However, investment in heavy industry accounted for 83 percent of the total investment in industry. Large capital-intensive factories with a high degree of mechanization were set up in the major industrial centres, following blueprints imported from the Soviet Union that set down the smallest operational details. No less than 10,000 Soviet experts and industrial advisers helped in the process.[12]

No doubt, the technological aid of the Soviet Union speeded up China's development, but it was not without undesirable side effects. Industrial development was concentrated in the major centres; local industries in the smaller urban centres and the rural areas were neglected. The development of small-scale industries ranked low on the government's list of priorities. Engaged in the production of simple tools, artistic goods, and services ancillary to industry, factories in the small-scale industries tended to be small, usually employing less than fifty workers, and were less mechanized. As pointed out by Carl Riskin,[13] the neglect of local industries led to an inadequate supply of agricultural equipment. Existing supplies were poor in quality, high in cost, and generally unsuited to peasant needs. Not only did this lead to growing disparity between the industrially advanced and the backward areas;[14] it also had repercussions on agricultural developments.

The basis of China's economy was agriculture. When the communists came to power, about 85 percent of the population was engaged in agriculture, with the rest belonging to the industrial or service sector.[15] However, the degree of mechanization in agriculture was low. Agricultural development was stunted by the ravages of foreign aggression and internal strife. Practically no farm machinery had been introduced in China prior to 1949, with the exception of farms established by the Japanese in Manchuria. In general, primitive locally made farm implements—wooden hoes, ploughs, and the like—were used. Transportation was also primitive and inefficient. A large proportion of goods was carried by wheelbarrow or by humans using shoulder poles. According to a survey carried out in 1954,

> each peasant owned an average of three mou of arable land, each household possessing less than fourteen mou. Other means of production were scarce. Taking the country as a whole, each peasant household had on an average less than one draught animal, every two households a plough, and every ten a water wheel. The poverty-stricken peasant often had no draught animal or large farm tools; even if they did possess a few tools they either needed repair or were of poor quality.[16]

Former landlords, however, were generally in a better position. Rich peasants had, on the average, two draught animals, a plough, and a water wheel shared with two others. Some even hired labourers to work on their farms.

While the state made some effort to raise the level of mechanization and production in agriculture, the main focus of economic policy in the early years was on heavy industry. State efforts in agriculture were mainly confined to the production of chemical fertilizers, but output was still low and the fertilizers produced were usually allotted to essential products, such as cotton, grown on state farms. The state also made an effort to popularize improved types of farm tools, such as double-single ploughs, walking ploughs, sprayers, and water wheels. By 1957, agricultural machinery stations had been established to lend out tractors and farm machines to the cooperatives, but with only 24,600 tractors available and a lack of trained technicians, the supply could not begin to meet demand.[17]

The result was a much slower rate of growth in agriculture as compared to industry. For example, agricultural output increased by only 3 percent in 1953, while industrial production was up by 30 percent in the same year. (See Table 7) This differential growth rate in industry and agriculture produced a fundamental

Table 7 Economic Growth of China 1949–57

Year	Combined Gross Output of Industry and Agriculture Value in Million Yuan	Industry		Agriculture	
		Value in Million Yuan	Percent of Combined Gross Value	Value in Million Yuan	Percent of Combined Gross Value
1949	46,610	14,020	30.01	32,590	69.99
1950	57,480	19,120	33.26	38,360	64.74
1951	68,320	26,350	38.57	41,970	61.43
1952	82,720	34,330	41.50	48,390	58.50
1953	94,610	44,700	47.25	49,910	52.75
1954	103,540	51,970	50.19	51,570	49.81
1955	110,410	54,870	50.00	55,540	50.00
1956	128,650	70,360	54.69	58,290	45.31
1957	138,740	78,390	56.50	60,350	43.50

Source: *Ten Great Years* (Peking: Foreign Languages Press, 1960), pp. 87, 118.

change in the economic base. Agriculture had accounted for 49 percent of the gross national product in 1952; it had dropped to about 39 percent in 1958. However, the slow pace of growth in agriculture also had its repercussions on industrial development. By 1955, industrial growth had dropped to 7.1 percent per annum. This the government attributed to the decline in farm output, especially the failure of industrial crops.[18]

Despite this weakness, China experienced a steady growth in her economy during these eight years after liberation. Economists differ in their estimates of China's production and development in this period, depending on their degree of confidence in Chinese official statistics. Estimates of her average annual growth rate may vary from 2 to 8 percent in agriculture, and from 14 to 19 percent in industry,[19] but whether one accepts the high or the low estimates, one still has to conclude that the years between 1949 and 1957 were a period of economic growth. It was this fact that generated the optimism which characterized the policies of the Great Leap Forward, 1958–59.

SOCIAL RELATIONS OF PRODUCTION

Together with technological advice, the Soviets also gave advice on how to manage industrial enterprises. One characteristic feature of the Soviet model of management is the reliance on material incentives. Wage differentials were maintained in China as in Russia to encourage workers to work harder and impel the rational use of labour by managers. Bonuses were paid to those who exceeded the output norms. In theory, bonuses were to be limited to 20 percent of the base wage, but in reality they often far exceeded this target. The net result was a widening wage spread between the workers and management. In 1957, senior management reportedly earned 560 yuan a month, nearly four times as much as the top-paid workers, who earned 150 yuan a month at most.[20]

Industries in China were organized on a hierarchical basis at this time, with workers at the bottom and managers and technical personnel above. Influenced by the Soviet model of one-man management, factory directors acquired complete authority and power over each production unit, down to the work team or section. Each unit was directly responsible to and closely supervised by the one above, the hierarchy of control and authority being very strictly defined. This ran counter to the Maoist philosophy of mass line, generated a special elite of managerial and technical staff, and further increased the gap between workers and management.

The Soviet model of scientific management also required detailed work plans for production and administration. These plans were based on exact measurements of mechanical, technical, and human performance; once formulated, such plans were followed precisely. However, hard data were difficult to obtain in the relatively primitive economic, technical, and administrative environment of China. Chinese industries were generally run on a loose organizational basis and traditional values and preferences conflicted with what would seem to be economically rational. Without such data, planning was hampered. The result was to encourage planners to seek low targets that they could easily meet or exceed, thus defeating the purpose of maximizing output.

While the social relations of production in industry thus followed a transplanted and alien model, the organization of agricultural production grew out of the requirements of the forces of production. The low level of technology in agriculture and the inadequate supply of draught animals and farm tools encouraged, as mentioned earlier, the formation of mutual aid teams, and later on, of cooperatives to pool resources. The formation of these cooperatives led in turn to greater mechanization, as the pooling of land and resources made feasible the use of agricultural machinery such as harvesters and tractors. Productivity was increased, as was the quality of life. The peasants could now plan and carry out larger-scale irrigation projects and build power plants to provide electricity for their own use. Unlike the organization of industry, that of agriculture was not a system imposed from above; it was a spontaneous development, with the initiative coming from the peasants. The mutual aid teams and cooperatives were usually formed with the encouragement and mobilization from the administrative cadres, but the final decision to unite rested with the individual peasant households concerned. Decisions concerning production and other projects were made by the elected representatives, in consultation with the members of the mutual aid teams or cooperatives. Often they were made directly by the members at large.

Much of the transformation that had taken place had been in the legal form of property ownership and the formal relations of production. A more basic contradiction, however, still persisted in the changeover to socialism from capitalism: the ideology of the capitalist social formation lingered. Its transformation and the weeding out of capitalist traits in the economic system still had to be carried out. This had to be done not only within the economic system, but through the ideological state apparatus, the most important part of which was the educational system. In the next chapter, we shall look at the efforts of the hegemonic group to transform the capitalist ideology of the masses into a socialist one.

Educational Development: 1949–1957

While the ownership of property had been transferred to the state through legislation, many of the underlying structures and ideological supports characteristic of the capitalist social formation lingered well into the late fifties. From the beginning of the establishment of the communist state, efforts were made to transform the ideological outlook of the masses. These often took the form of rectification campaigns waged by wall posters, the newspapers, and the different units against bureaucracy, corruption, speculation, and other aspects of bourgeois thought. But the more sustained drive to transform the ideology of the population was through the educational system. A multiplicity of ways was used to bring educational facilities to the bulk of China's population, among them being spare-time schools, broadcasting schools, correspondence schools, and short-term schools; however, we shall concentrate on the formal school system.

THE SCHOOL SYSTEM IN CHINA: OPEN VS ELITIST SYSTEM

The educational system inherited by the communists in 1949 was organized along the American pattern, with six years of primary school, three years of junior high school, three years of senior high school, and three to five years of university, depending on the subject. At the high school level, there were three basic types of schooling offered: academic high school, normal school for the training of teachers, and vocational or technical school. At the university level, there were composite universities and more specialized institutes of higher learning. The composite universities were interdisciplinary, in the sense that they embraced both arts and sciences; their function was to strengthen the theoretical foundations of higher learning and prepare the students to teach and do research. The other institutions of higher learning provided facilities for professional training, and included faculties for teacher training and colleges specializing in petroleum, mining, oil refining, and agriculture.[1]

The age of the students ranged from seven to thirteen in primary schools, and fourteen to nineteen in secondary schools. The age of those in the universities was from about nineteen to twenty-six. In 1949, according to the last statistics of the nationalist regime, there were 207 universities and institutes of higher learning with 155,306 students, 5,892 secondary schools with 1,878,528 students, and 290,617 primary schools with 23,813,705 students. That is, less than 20 percent of the population of school age were enrolled in school.[2]

Before 1949, schools and universities were run either by the nationalist government or by private individuals and missionary groups. When the communists came to power, they took over control of the nationalist schools; then, in 1952, all private schools were brought under government control.

The primary and secondary schools were put under local departments or boards of education, but their degree of control over the schools varied directly with their distance from them. Many of the local boards of education were situated in urban areas. The farther the schools were from the administrative centres, the greater was their autonomy. The universities, on the other hand, came under the dual control of the Ministry of Higher Education and the ministry they would provide with manpower; for example, institutes of agriculture would be under the joint control of the ministries of both higher education and agriculture. This practice is an indicator of the emphasis the hegemonic group put on the role of higher education in meeting the needs of the various branches of the economy.

The government takeover of all schools ensured that the educational system would serve the needs of the general population. One of its aims was to expand and universalize the system. This meant the extension of educational facilities from the existing 20 percent to the remaining 80 percent of the school-age population.

To this end, the government allotted a sizable proportion of the budget to education. It was roughly 7 percent from 1950 to 1956. In 1957, even though the total budget decreased by 4 percent, that

**Table 8   Enrolment in Educational Institutes in China 1949–58
(Numbers in Thousands)**

School Year	Primary	Secondary General	University
1949–50	24,391	1,039	117
1950–51	28,924	1,305	137
1951–52	43,154	1,568	153
1952–53	51,100	2,490	191
1953–54	51,664	2,933	212
1954–55	51,218	3,587	253
1955–56	53,126	3,900	288
1956–57	63,464	5,165	403
1957–58	64,279	6,281	441

Source: *Ten Great Years* (Peking: Foreign Languages Press, 1960),
    p. 192.

for education increased by 10 percent. According to government statistics enrolment in primary schools increased nearly three times between 1950 and 1958. In the same period, enrolment in the secondary schools increased five times, and in higher education, four times. Overall, there was an increase of 300 percent in enrolment between 1950 and 1957. By the end of 1957, about 40 percent of the school-age population (about 189 million) was receiving an education.[3] Some of these figures might be exaggerated. Given the determined effort of the government and the innovativeness of the different measures used, the rise in enrolment must have been spectacular.

The state wanted especially to 'open doors to peasants and workers', that is, to extend the educational facilities to the worker/ peasant class, who had traditionally been deprived of education.[4] In 1951, the minister of education reported that in the 'old' areas (those that were controlled by the communists before liberation), the offspring of workers and peasants made up 80 percent of the total number of middle and elementary school students.[5] National data on the percentage of students of working-class and peasant origins at these levels are not available, but it seems likely to be

**Table 9 Students of Worker-Peasant Origin in
Higher Educational Institutes in China**

School Year	Number	Percentage of Total
1952–53	40,000	20.46
1955–56	80,000	29.20
1956–57	130,000	34.29
1957–58	160,000	36.42

Source: *Peking Review* 1 (September 1958), 27:10.

lower. At the university level, it is estimated that students from these backgrounds accounted for 20.5 percent of the total enrolment in 1953 and 34.3 percent in 1957.[6] In spite of this increase, these students are under-represented when conservative estimates would put their percentage in the population at large at over 80 percent. It seems that higher education, at least, remained the fairly exclusive preserve of intellectuals, professionals, cadres, and rich peasants. And among the peasant/worker class, those of working-class origin would be in a better position to benefit from the universities, since these were usually situated in the urban areas.

Universities and secondary schools tended to cluster in the towns and cities. Of the 200 odd universities in China in the early fifties, a quarter were in Shanghai[7] and another quarter in or near Peking.[8] Secondary schools were more evenly distributed throughout the country, but students from the rural areas still had to board or travel long distances daily if they wanted to attend, and though some villages had their own primary schools, peasants living in more remote areas still had to travel several miles to neighbouring villages to attend school.

Government policy in this period did not alleviate the disparity. To a certain extent, it even accentuated it. With the adoption of the First Five Year Plan, the government attached greater importance to the development of technical high schools than to primary and general high schools; moreover, their efforts went to extend such schools in the larger cities and industrial and mining districts rather than in the districts where industry was less developed.[9] The urban population clearly had a greater advantage than the rural one.

In the early fifties, the American influence that had been evident during the nationalist period was replaced by the Russian one. In certain areas, the government tried to adopt the Soviet system of ten-year schooling, but it was soon given up, perhaps because of opposition from the bureaucracy, which met attempts to institute any radical change with resistance, if not opposition. Most of the bureaucracy had been educated along the American system. To them, education represented a means not only of training manpower, but of certifying and legitimizing one's qualifications and position. It may be that they saw a changeover from the American system to the Russian one as jeopardizing their own positions.

Another reason for the failure to devote adequate attention to overhauling the educational system may have been the preoccupation of the policy-makers with national reconstruction and economic recovery. The reforms suggested in the major policy statements of the time[10] included the extension of existing educational facilities, the re-education of existing teaching staff, the training of more teachers, the reform of the curriculum, the simplification of the written language, and a more centralized system of control. There is little indication of concern with restructuring the classroom, the teaching methods, or the school system. Indeed, available documents on educational policies in the early fifties indicate a preoccupation with fitting the communist ideology into the existing system.

The hegemonic group did recognize that the educational system prior to liberation was a capitalist one. In 1951, the *People's Daily* described the former system in these terms: 'The school system of old China was an imitation of the system of capitalist states and reflected the reactionary ideology of landlords, bureaucrats, and the compradore class of semi-colonial, semi-feudal society. ... The labouring people had no position in the culture and education of old China.'[11] The irony is that the hegemonic group felt that the piecemeal changes mentioned above were adequate to resolve the contradictions between the socialist and capitalist educational systems and transform the system to a socialist one. This complacency was clearly reflected in the proceedings of the National Secondary Education Conference in

1954, which closed with the resolution that the 'future problem of the existing schools is not one of remolding but one of progress and development.'[12]

 In effect, the retention of traditional educational structures worked against the equalization of educational opportunities. The admission procedures in particular tended to preserve the monopoly of a traditional elite in the educational system. Decisions for admission were based on the applicants' physical fitness, their social status, their political background, and their academic performance. A great deal of emphasis was put on the result of the entrance examination based on the school syllabus. Only one-third of the primary school graduates could enter secondary schools, and only one-sixth of the high school graduates could enter university. (See Table 8) Competition was therefore keen and tended to favour those already most advantaged. Children of proletarian origin traditionally took time from school to help in productive work, whereas the living conditions of those of bourgeois origin were more conducive to study for this type of examination. Children of bourgeois origin also generally attended the better equipped urban schools, which were staffed by better-qualified teachers than those of the rural areas, and usually obtained superior grades. So long as they or their parents had not collaborated with the KMT or the Japanese, they would not be discriminated against because of their political background. When students of proletarian origin were admitted to the universities, they were sometimes handicapped by the training they had received in their former schools. Their dropout rate was probably high.

For the foregoing reasons, education remained largely the preserve of the traditional elite, in spite of the tremendous rate of expansion in education in the early fifties. It was the intellectuals, professionals, or rich peasants, and petty bourgeoisie who were most able to benefit from the increased facilities. The rest were still at a disadvantage, although urban workers found it easier than the rural peasantry to make use of the schools.

CURRICULUM WITHIN THE SCHOOL SYSTEM

Prior to 1952, there was little standardization in the school curriculum. Every province, and sometimes individual schools, had their own textbooks. Together with the movement towards central planning in the economic sector and the impetus to bring the schools under government control, the government made an organized attempt to standardize the textbooks. This was also part of a program to unify the Chinese spoken language and to simplify the written language by using less complex Chinese characters. Books were rewritten and compiled by the Ministry of Education. The schools in the country were to choose their texts from the list of books compiled. While such measures helped to make educational standards more uniform and to weed out any bourgeois ideology that might be present in school texts, they also generated problems and had some undesirable defects.

According to the ideology embodied in the thoughts of Mao Tse-tung, the curriculum should be relevant to local needs and conditions. But it is inconceivable that a curriculum formulated at the national level could be relevant to the needs of every region. Indeed, the curriculum had a strong urban bias. The peasants found many examples in the textbooks outside the scope of their everyday experience and irrelevant to their daily life. This difficulty was accentuated by the strong Russian influence that existed throughout the early fifties. In a deliberate attempt to learn from the Soviet Union, the Chinese systematically translated Soviet material and used the Soviet curriculum as a blueprint, regardless of regional and national differences. In a grade 4 textbook published in 1957, for example, six out of forty lessons were translated from Russian, and used Russian names and settings.[13]

An indication of the priority the government put on raising the level of technology in the economy is the fivefold increase in the educational budget for scientific development between 1955 and 1956. The amount spent on university and secondary education also continued to increase in 1956, whereas the budget for primary education was cut by 18 percent.[14] This again reflected the policy-makers' concern with developing manpower at the middle and higher levels to facilitate the development of heavy industry. Enrolment in engineering at the university level increased from one-quarter to about three-eighths of the total enrolment between 1950 and 1958, while the percentage of students in agriculture remained stable, reflecting the lower priority assigned it. The proportion of students in such liberal arts as literature, law, and political science declined from one-fifth to one-tenth of the stu-

Table 10 Higher Education: Enrolment by Field as Percentage of Total 1949–58

School Year	Engineering	Science	Agriculture and Forestry	Health	Political Science and Law	Education	Finance and Economics	Liberal Arts	Total
1949–50	26.0	6.0	8.9	13.0	6.3	10.6	16.7	12.5	100
1950–51	27.8	—	—	12.5	—	9.6	—	—	100
1951–52	31.2	—	—	13.8	—	11.7	—	—	100
1952–53	34.8	5.0	8.1	12.9	2.0	16.7	11.5	9.0	100
1953–54	37.7	5.8	7.2	13.7	1.8	19.4	6.4	8.0	100
1954–55	37.5	6.8	6.3	13.4	1.6	21.8	4.4	8.2	100
1955–56	38.1	6.9	7.5	12.7	1.7	21.9	3.9	7.3	100
1956–57	36.8	6.3	—	—	—	24.3	—	—	100
1957–58	40.9	6.2	8.6	12.6	2.1	21.3	2.9	5.4	100

Source: Leo A. Orleans, *Professional Manpower and Education in Communist China* (Washington: National Science Foundation, 1960), p. 71.

dent population in the same period. (See Table 10) Since the quotas on enrolment were set by the government according to its estimation of the economic needs of the country, these changes were the result of definite government policy.

During this period, the emphasis on practice in the acquisition of knowledge and ideological education in socialist reconstruction was largely neglected. The integration of theory with practice was adhered to only in the technical schools and universities of engineering or agriculture. Even here, however, this principle meant simply a closer coordination between these institutes and the relevant government departments in their research endeavours, and not the introduction of productive labour or practical application of studies into the curriculum.[15] In general, it remained academically oriented. This bias could be found even at the lower educational levels. In the primary schools, a student learnt six subjects in the first four years; in the last two years, nature studies, geography, and physical education were added. Out of the twenty-four periods per week in the junior primary schools, twenty were spent on language and arithmetic.[16] In the secondary schools, there was a distinct emphasis on linguistics, science, and mathematics. In extracurricular activities, the bias toward academic studies also continued. For example, among such youth organizations as the Young Pioneers—though the motto was to be 'good in work, study, body, thinking, and labour'—the activities commonly reported were study sessions held under politically advanced teachers. Academic orientation remained the chief criterion for admission into such organizations.

Ideological education was confined to the re-education of the teaching staff; for the younger generation it was completely ignored. In the rules of conduct for primary and secondary school, students were exhorted to be obedient, punctual, respectful, quiet, orderly, well-behaved, diligent, polite, friendly, and honest.[17] Indeed, these rules of conduct would fit well into any society, capitalist or socialist; none can be distinguished as being specifically geared to the young of a socialist society.

The neglect of the ideological aspects of education at this time perhaps represented an oversight on the part of the policymakers. It also demonstrates the lag between ideology and its reification in social structures. In theory, education was recognized as playing an important role in socializing the young, but in practice, perhaps as a result of capitalist influences on the members of the hegemonic group themselves, greater emphasis was placed on the role of education in training technical manpower for socialist reconstruction. Members of the hegemonic group at this time were more concerned with national reconstruction than with changes in the educational structure that would facilitate ideological change. The result was a disparity between education and the economy. The economy had become largely socialist with the transformation of the property relations of production, but the educational system retained its pre-liberation capitalist form, disputing the simplistic assumption that the ideological superstructure is necessarily a mirror image of the economic base.

It is also possible that the hegemonic group believed that ideological transformation of the population could be more effectively handled by mass campaigns, such as the 'Land Reform Campaign', the 'Resist American and Aid Korea Campaign', 'Suppression of Counter Revolutionaries', 'the Three-Anti Five-Anti Campaign', and the 'Hundred Flowers Movement'.[18] Each of these campaigns, which were launched in the early fifties to transform the outlook of the population, had its individual focus. The purposes of the first three campaigns are self-evident. The 'Three-Anti Five-Anti Campaign' was directed against corruption, waste, and bureaucracy among the government employees, and also against bribery, tax evasion, theft of state property, cheating on government contracts, and stealing economic information for speculation among business men. The 'Hundred Flowers Movement' started in the mid-fifties, when the government encouraged individuals to articulate their opinions on, and make suggestions to improve, existing government measures. However, many of the criticisms were openly hostile to the government, and it ended as a rectification campaign against those who had expressed their subversive ideas. The delegation to the masses of the campaign for ideological transformation may have arisen from sheer practical considerations, since the educational system was dominated by people who would oppose the introduction of such programs into the schools. How much simpler and more efficient, then, to put pressure on these entrenched elites through campaigns that reached the whole of society!

Whatever the intention of the campaigns, the pre-capitalist educational system remained intact and in the hands of the traditional elites, especially at the bureaucratic level. The curriculum emphasized academic studies rather than the 'unity of theory and practice'. Ideological education and participation in labour were only nominally part of the curriculum, thus limiting the effectiveness of the educational system as an ideological instrument of the socialist state. It became increasingly evident in the mid-sixties that all this had a detrimental influence on the younger generation and that a radical overhaul of the system was needed. In the meantime, only piecemeal reforms in education were introduced.

PART ★ TWO

*Changing Economy and
the Struggle for Educational
Change*

★6★

The Great Leap Forward: 1958–1959

The years 1958–59 have a certain unity of their own in the context of China's struggle for a new social order. The period is commonly known as the Great Leap Forward (GLF) when China surged forth with renewed impatience for development.

On the eve of 1958, economic conditions looked very promising. The nine years since liberation had been a time of uninterrupted growth in industry and agriculture even though development in agriculture lagged behind that of industry. The property relationship had been transformed with the transfer of ownership of property to the state. In agriculture, cooperatives had become relatively widespread. It was in this atmosphere of optimism that the draft Second Five Year Plan (SFYP) was launched to accelerate growth in agriculture.

In education, it was also a period of growth. Enrolment in schools had increased threefold in the past nine years. However, the disparity in enrolment between the urban and rural areas persisted. Even though there was an increasing emphasis on political education by the policy-makers, the structure of the school system and its activities still retained many of the characteristics of pre-liberation times, including its emphasis on academic achievement.

GOALS OF THE GREAT LEAP FORWARD: REACTIONS TO CHANGING OBJECTIVE REALITY

The draft Second Five Year Plan, passed in the Eighth National Congress in September 1956, pushed for the further expansion of China's economy on a socialist basis. Its goals were:

(1) to continue industrial construction with heavy industries as its core, promote technical reconstruction of the national economy, and build a solid foundation for socialist industrialization;

(2) to carry through socialist transformation, and consolidate and expand the system of ownership by the whole people; (3) to further increase the production of industry, agriculture, and handicrafts and correspondingly develop transport and commerce on the basis of developing capitalist construction and carry through socialist transformation; (4) to make vigorous efforts to train personnel for construction work and strengthen scientific research to meet the needs of the development of socialist economy and culture; and (5) to reinforce the national defences and raise the people's material and cultural life on the basis of increased industrial and agricultural production.[1]

The targets of the draft SFYP and those finally adopted in 1958 were very similar. The policies adopted in the years 1958–59 were embodied in the slogans 'general line' and the 'GLF'. These terms, often used interchangeably, referred to the simultaneous development of socialist construction and socialist revolution, and the transformation of agriculture, handicraft industries, and capitalist industries into socialist ones. The general line referred more to the general direction of development and the GLF more to the specific issues of achieving 'greater, faster, better, and more economic results in a simultaneous development of industry and agriculture, heavy industries, and light industry'.[2]

The attention given to agriculture in this period arose out of a growing awareness of weaknesses that had resulted from the exclusive attention devoted to heavy industry in the early fifties. Agricultural production lagged behind industrial development. Food grain production had increased by only 3.7 percent, barely keeping up with the rate of population growth.[3] In 1957, Mao said:

Because of the good harvests of 1952 and 1955, the development of the national economy was quite rapid in 1953 and 1956. ... Because the 1954 and 1956 harvests were bad, the development of the national economy was rather slow in 1955 and 1957. ... The reason is that 80 percent of the materials needed by our country's light industry depend on agriculture, and light industry constitutes about 50 percent of the relative weight of all our industry.[4]

In other words, Mao recognized that agricultural output during one year influenced the industrial output of the next.

Mao's plea to develop agriculture did not represent any significant departure from the emphasis on heavy industry laid down in the draft FFYP and SFYP. At the sixth plenum of the Eighth Central Committee of the Chinese Communist Party (CCPCC) in November 1958, it was clearly stated that the policy was to be one of 'simultaneous development of industry and agriculture on the basis of giving priority to heavy industry'. The development of heavy industry was regarded as the key to 'the successful technical transformation of all other departments of the economy'.[5] Development in agriculture was to ensure the uninterrupted development in industry.

The major aims of the GLF did not differ to any great extent from those of the FFYP and the SFYP, except that there was a greater emphasis on the role of agriculture in facilitating industrial growth and a greater impatience to move towards the goals of socialist revolution and construction.

STRATEGIES OF DEVELOPMENT: AN ISSUE OF GREAT DEBATE

While the aims of the FFYP, SFYP, and GLF were relatively similar, there were essential differences between the strategies of the GLF and those embodied in both the First and Second Five Year plans.

The draft SFYP followed the Russian model of development. After laying down the targets for the development of heavy industry, light industry, and agriculture, the draft SFYP suggested that China 'should energetically develop scientific research, with emphasis on particular subjects in accordance with the need of national construction'.[6] It advocated the retention of material incentives and a free market, at least for the time being. In the words of the vice premier, Ch'en Yun,

> We should either use the method of selective purchasing by state commercial departments or allow the producers to market their own products. A large number of small factories should continue to operate independently, while handicrafts cooperatives should be split into smaller ones with the compo-

nent teams or households managed separately. Members of agricultural cooperatives should be allowed to take up different kinds of subsidiary occupations of their own. Minor local products should be freed from market control.[7]

He envisaged that after adoption of these measures, there would be a greater supply of better quality consumer goods.

In accordance with this perception of development in strong economic terms, the supporters of the SFYP saw education mainly as a method to develop technology to meet national needs. Chou En-lai stated in his report on the proposals of the SFYP:

It is the foremost task of education to train the state personnel for the work of construction, especially industrial technicians and personnel for scientific research. ... Therefore in the SFYP period, we should further develop our higher education and secondary vocational education. ... We must pay due consideration to the relation between numbers and quality. In the past few years, we have put undue emphasis on numbers and neglected quality; this is a tendency that must be corrected. Educational institutions should do their utmost to increase the number of students as far as possible on condition that their quality is ensured to a certain extent.[8]

With this emphasis on the goal of education to serve technology and national construction, improvement of academic quality was given priority over expansion and ideological education.

The chief spokesmen of the SFYP were Ch'en Yun, the vice premier and first secretary of the Economics and Finance Committee, Chou En-lai, the premier, and Teng Tzu-hui, the director of the Department of Rural Work. Information on the other supporters of the SFYP is lacking. Mao's report on agricultural development, which warned of the growing rifts in Chinese society between rich and poor, the urban and the rural population, was ignored, indicating that supporters of the SFYP were at this time in the majority. However, this situation did not last.

The 'Hundred Flowers Movement' (January 1956–mid-1957) had released a flood of criticism of both the Communist Party and its policies. Some of this criticism was subversive and anti-communist.[9] But some revealed genuine weaknesses within the system, the low general level of understanding of communism, especially among the intellectuals, and the weaknesses of 'leaning to one side' (that is, in the context of strong dependence on Soviet aid); the growing bureaucratization, the workstyle of the cadres, the tendency to extravagance, and the wasting of local resources. Pan Shu, former president of the University of Nanking, for example, criticized the government's educational policy in these terms:

> In the past few years, I think, we have not attached sufficient importance to our own experts, nor have we fully availed ourselves of their talents. This has resulted in great losses in our work and has also seriously hampered the initiative of our own experts. ... In many cases, the Ministry of Higher Education tried to learn from the Soviet Union in a blind mechanical way. So far as the course of psychology is concerned, the Ministry of Higher Education because it blindly followed the Soviet pattern, decided to place this course [psychology] in the curricula of the department of philosophy. ... True, in the Soviet Union, the course of psychology is placed in the curricula of the philosophy department. But this is merely due to old traditions, and therefore there is no good reason for it.[10]

This outpouring of criticism revealed a great deal of dissatisfaction over following the Soviet pattern of development and dependence on Soviet aid, and pointed to the necessity both for making better use of existing local resources and for more ideological reforms.

The weaknesses in existing policies brought out during the 'Hundred Flowers Movement' and the assessment of economic conditions resulted in a reassessment of the strategies of development incorporated in the SFYP and a realignment of the forces within the decision-making group. It led to a changeover from support for the SFYP to the Maoist line of the GLF. In 1958, Liu Shao-ch'i had defended the Maoist line of the GLF against those who 'wondered whether the implementation of the policy of consistently achieving greater, faster, better, and more economic results would not lead to waste ... throw the various branches of production off balance, as well as divert some funds which could be used by the state for industrialization'. This defence, given in conjunction with the announcement of the general line, indicated that opposition at that time was great. Liu announced the 'necessity to build socialism by exerting ... utmost efforts, and pressing ahead consistently to achieve greater, faster, better, and more economic results'.[11] However, by that time, the policies of the GLF seem to have obtained the support of the majority of the decision-makers. Among the twenty-eight members of the Politburo, ten came out with statements in support of the GLF. They were K'o Ch'ing-shih, K'ang Sheng, Liu Shao-ch'i, Tan Chen-lin, Po I-po, Lu Ting-i, Ch'en Po-ta, Mao Tse-tung, and Ulanfu.[12]

Though the members of the Politburo and the central state apparatus gave their support to the policies of the GLF, they did not have identical views and interests. Among those involved in education, for example, Chiang Nan-hsiang and Lu Ting-i supported the Maoist educational line, but they put greater emphasis on technical and scientific research than did Mao. At this particular juncture, Liu was allied with Mao, but his statements preached more 'restraint' than did Mao's. Chou, together with Ch'en Yun and Teng Tzu-hui, the main spokesmen of the SFYP, remained relatively silent through this period; however, differences among these three existed as well. Chou's statements[13] did not indicate that he supported the others' emphasis on material incentives and the free market.

What were in the policies of the GLF that warranted such debate even though its goals were similar to those of the SFYP? The First and Second Five Year plans were based on the Soviet model of development, while the policy of the GLF was the first attempt since 1949 to deviate from it and to develop a model more suited to Chinese conditions. It was more akin to the prototype developed during the Yenan Period. The FFYP and the SFYP emphasized the development of above-norm projects, using capital-intensive methods, Soviet aid, and concentrating development in a few industrial centres. Under the GLF, the targets were to be fulfilled by 'walking on two legs' and self-sufficiency. Instead of relying exclusively on Soviet aid and capital-intensive projects, China was to depend on mass mobilization. Instead of developing only a few industrial centres, industrialization was to spread to the countryside. In the call for the increased production of iron and steel, for example, the target of production was 18 million tons in 1959, of which about 30 to 40 percent was to come from local iron and steel furnaces.[14] Locally produced iron and steel was to be used in the production of 'farm implements for local needs, machinery, carts, ball bearings, and improvised machine tools' for agricultural use. Light industry was also to be developed in the countryside for the production of consumer goods; making starch, processing food and flax; pressing oil; making paper, cloth, bricks, and tiles.[15] Through the development of heavy and light industry, using capital-intensive methods and advanced technology on the one hand, and mass mobilization and local resources on the other, the hegemonic group hoped China would attain self-sufficiency and lessen its dependence on Soviet aid. It also hoped to equalize the rate of development in industry and agriculture and rectify differences in the level of development between the urban and rural areas.

One result of the revelations of extravagance during the 'Hundred Flowers Movement' and the adoption of the policy of maximizing local resources was the launching of anti-waste and anti-conservative campaigns.

In June 1958, the State Council issued a directive on the procurement and utilization of waste materials: 'In the past years, the state procured only part of the materials left unused. Part of what was procured was not fully utilized.... We must strenuously organize the mass forces to collect extensively and utilize fully those waste materials, so as to support the development of industrial and agricultural production in a better way, thus serving to realize the Party's general line of socialist construction.'[16] This campaign involved the collection of scrap parts and unused materials for recycling, the cutting of administrative expenses, and the sending of cadres to the lower levels to help local development and reduce administrative costs.

The anti-conservative campaign was an attempt to mobilize the masses through ideological education. Such attempts had been carried out through various media since liberation, but among the peasants, traces of superstition remained. When a day was regarded as unpropitious for making a journey, they did not leave home. When a day was unfavourable for breaking the earth, they did not break the earth. Peasants now worked side by side with the intellectuals and the experts who helped them to understand and overcome the environment and to root out superstition. Among the intellectuals, there were ideological problems of another nature. They had too much faith in the prowess of the West, in particular of the United States, Britain, and France. During the anti-conservative campaign, the intellectuals were sent to the grass-roots level to integrate with the masses, to learn their wisdom and to appreciate their contribution. It was also an anti-bureaucratization measure to draw the administrative cadres closer to the masses. Local scientific research centres were set up for this purpose, and to capitalize on local resources and attain the Maoist concept of self-sufficiency utilizing mass mobilization.

Another departure from the Russian model was the policy of decentralization. Instead of relying on central planning and one-man management, planning now came under local control and involved mass participation. On August 29, the CCPCC resolution for the establishment of a larger number of the communes was passed. The creation of these decentralized clusters of decision-making groups, working within broad policy guidelines, was expected to minimize communication costs and administrative expenses and to facilitate a more effective mobilization of resources than would have been possible under a bureaucratic, centralized system. While such an administrative style certainly more closely reflected Maoist ideology, this feature seems to have been downplayed. Rather, it was publicized that the communes represented a further advance towards communism, in that property would be owned by the collective and the distribution of products would no longer be made according to a person's contribution in land and labour, but according to basic needs.

The establishment of the communes also represented an accommodation to changing objective conditions within the confines of the hegemonic ideology. The communes were to be made up of a larger number of households than the cooperatives. This pooling of resources among a greater number of households made possible a more rational utilization of resources for the simultaneous development of light industry, agricultural improvement, and iron and steel production. In addition, according to Schurmann, the establishment of the first commune did not originate from the centre; it arose out of a reaction to local conditions.

One gets the impression that the leaders were receiving information rather than handing out suggestions and policy statements. ... We would like to suggest that the July high tide [referring to the communes] may have erupted in Honan, Manchuria, and a few other places without an explicit order to that effect from Peking. If so, it would explain these far-ranging visits of almost all the top leaders in Peking. Ever sensitive to the delicate situation, they apparently wanted to see with their own eyes what was transpiring. What they saw evidently pleased them.[17]

Indeed, as we shall see later, many of the movements and campaigns in China arose out of local initiative. There was a constant interaction between the implementation and the decision-making levels, objective conditions, and individual initiative. Innovations came about as a response to real needs, and when they were conducive to socialist development, and came to the attention of the hegemonic group, they would be given due notice and publicity and incorporated as policies to be implemented throughout the country.

EDUCATIONAL POLICY AND ITS RELATIONSHIP TO ECONOMIC POLICY

The hegemonic group in China clearly recognized the reciprocal role between education and the economy. On the one hand, they recognized the supportive role of education in the reproduction of the economic structure, the transformation of the ideology of its agents, and the dissemination of technical skills. Educational changes had to be carried out in response to changing economic requirements; the educational changes in turn played an active role in transforming the old economic structure into a new one. A joint directive of the CCPCC and the State Council, issued in 1958, read in part:

The Great Leap Forward in industrial and agricultural production has brought about the beginning of an upsurge in the cultural revolution, characterized in the main by the rapid expansion of a literacy campaign and educational and cultural work. One of the great historical tasks now confronting the whole party and the people is to train tens of millions of red and expert intellectuals of the working class by giving correct leadership in educational work, by firmly adhering to the party line in educational development....Education is one of the powerful tools for transforming the old and building up a new society ... it serves the socialist revolution, the building of socialism and the communist revolution, which seeks to eliminate the remnants of all exploiting classes and systems of exploitation, the difference between cities and countryside, and the difference between mental and physical labour.[18]

The goals of economic development had remained relatively stable over the years, but there had been shifts in the priorities and strategies of economic development. Similar shifts could be detected in the educational policy. Chou En-lai's educational proposal, given in conjunction with the SFYP, had emphasized the quality of education, the training of experts, and the development of higher and vocational secondary education. With the adoption of the policies of the GLF, the main thrust of educational policies was now to equalize the rural-urban disparity and to restructure the educational system in line with the educational thoughts of Mao. The emphasis turned to (1) the expansion of educational facilities and (2) the acquisition of the proletarian outlook. Not that the acquisition of such an outlook had been previously ignored or that, during the GLF, educational institutions had ceased to train technical personnel; the training of 'red and expert' intellectuals remained the ideal to be striven for throughout the period. However, while the pursuits of 'redness' and expertise were not necessarily incompatible, the emphasis on one was usually to the detriment of the other.

In the face of limited financial and manpower resources for education, a two-pronged approach was introduced in 1958 to universalize and expand educational facilities throughout China. This was to be carried out through regular (full-time) and irregular (work/study and spare-time) schools. Full-time schools were state-financed and modelled after those established at the turn of the century. Work/study schools were mainly those set up by the various local units where students could divide their time between production and study. The purpose of participation in production work was to cut down the cost of running the school, to provide opportunities for students to acquire the proletarian outlook, and to put the theories they had learnt into practice. Spare-time schools had been widely used since the establishment of the People's Republic. Their main purpose was to raise the cultural level of working adults and to give technical training that would increase their contribution to production. An educated working class was especially necessary if workers were to take part in the decentralized method of decision-making.

The strategies used to universalize education were reminiscent of those used on the economic front as well as those of the Yenan Period—the maximum utilization of existing resources and mass mobilization. All forms of schools, including the regular full-time, spare-time, adult, nursery, and work/study schools, were to be used simultaneously. Not only would the state take up the responsibility in the provision of education; local units such as communes, mines, and factories were also expected to provide educational facilities.

In aid of the other goal of educational policy during this period— the acquisition of the proletarian outlook—teachers and students engaged in studies of Marxist-Leninist political and ideological writings so that they would acquire the 'viewpoint of the working-class, the mass viewpoint, the collective viewpoint, the labour viewpoint, or the viewpoint calling for the integration of mental with physical labour, and the dialectical materialist viewpoint'. Every student was to 'spend a certain period of the time in manual labour'.[19] Productive labour was listed as a formal course.

These policies not only represented initiatives from the centre to bring the existing educational system in closer conformity to the Maoist educational ideals, they also represented a summing up of experiences in the localities. Agricultural middle schools run on a work/study basis were one of the main thrusts of the directive. These schools started in Kiangsu before they were ever sanctioned by the centre. In March 1958, only two were known to exist in the province. In April, a conference summing up their experience was attended by Lu Ting-i, the director of propaganda, and as a result, their achievements were publicized throughout the whole nation. Agricultural schools were widely built in the following months. In August, another conference of teacher representatives from the agricultural middle schools was held. It was only in September that the work/study agricultural schools were mentioned in official educational policy statements. As in the case of the establishment of the communes, the initiative came from the provinces; the call from the centre only gave these schools the confirmation of official approval, which speeded up the process of development.

It is interesting to note that in the joint directive issued by the CCPCC and the State Council in September 1958, which embodied the educational policies of the GLF, there was a clause contradicting the spirit of this directive in the pursuit of equality, the elimination of differences between the country and the cities. It read:

> Among these ... schools, some are charged with the task of raising the educational level. These schools must have complete courses, and pay attention to raising the quality of their teaching and scientific research, as well as the different branches of study. Without jeopardizing their present standard of achievement, these schools should exert themselves to help in the building of schools. Any lowering of the standard of achievement in these schools, however, has a harmful effect on the cause of education as a whole.[20]

This clause encouraged many of the regular schools to interpret their task as that of keeping and raising academic standards. In a classless society, where the hierarchy of the social relations of production has been abolished, where there are no special prerogatives and status attached to different kinds of schools, and where access to schooling is universal, such divisions in the function of the schools might be acceptable, but in China at this time, the hierarchy in the social relations of production remained. One's status still depended mainly on one's educational qualifications and occupation. Regular schools were usually located in the urban areas, whereas the irregular schools were in the rural areas. Because of the special function of the regular schools, attending them offered the only channel of mobility if one aspired to higher education and higher status. As a result, even though the 1958 educational directive did, in general, serve to universalize education and raise the cultural and technical level of the masses in the rural areas, the inequality between the regular and irregular schools and the urban and the rural areas was perpetuated. This was to become a major issue during the Cultural Revolution.

The internal contradiction in the directive was probably an oversight on the part of the decision-makers, most of whom, as we pointed out in chapter 2, were educated in the pre-liberation period. Even though they were members of the Communist Party, Kuo Mo-jo, Lu Ting-i, and Chiang Nan-hsiang, and many other leaders in education, continued to put great emphasis on technical education and the training of the experts. They failed to realize that, given existing conditions in China, the pursuit of expertise, while not in itself anti-communist, would encourage capitalist tendencies and lead to the creation of a new class, if pursued without restraint. On the other hand, opposition to the policy of the GLF during this period certainly existed. A complete overhaul of the existing educational system to serve socialist development would have raised strong opposition at the centre. Judging from the criticisms that came out of the 'Hundred Flowers Movement', it was also unlikely that the country at large was ready to accept a complete overhaul of the existing system. This inconsistency of policies was perhaps a compromise to accommodate the diverse expectations.

The formulation of the educational policies at the centre involved a complex process of interaction between the ideology of the decision-makers and objective conditions—coming up with their aims for development, their strategies for economic development, their goals and conflicting strategies for educational development, their assessment of existing educational alternatives, their evaluations of a particular policy's feasibility in the existing conditions, and its acceptance by their fellow decision-makers. Educational policies were formulated as responses to the goals and strategies of economic development. The ideology of the policy-makers provided the framework whereby economic and educational goals and strategies were identified. In addition, the policy alternatives were circumscribed by the perception of the limitations of the objective conditions.

After the policies were formulated at the individual level, the acceptance of formal policy guidelines with or without modification depended on the sources of support among the decision-makers. Much depended on the policy's appeal to various class interests. The socialist nature of the educational policy of the GLF won the overall support of the decision-makers who condoned socialist ideology. The amount of support it commanded depended to a certain extent, as well, on the perceived efficiency of the proposed policy in overcoming weaknesses inherent in existing ones.

TRANSMISSION OF EDUCATIONAL DIRECTIVES

Educational directives from the centre did not come in the form of specific orders detailing the targets to be achieved, or the steps to be adopted. They were vague by western standards, and pointed only to the direction to be taken. Details and the concrete steps to be taken were to be worked out by the localities. This approach was especially pronounced during 1958 and 1959 when the movement was towards decentralization.

When a directive was announced at the centre, it was usually reported in the national newspapers, *Kuang-ming Daily* or the *People's Daily* and was widely reproduced in the local ones. In addition, study sessions would be carried out around these directives. Sometimes the policy was not transmitted in the form of a directive from the CCPCC or the State Council, but as an editorial of the *People's Daily* which would be widely quoted in the local newspapers. These editorials would be seriously studied at the local units by the cadres and the masses. For example, when the socialist line of national construction was passed at the second session of the Eighth CCPCC, there was great publicity. It was reported by the New China News Agency that in May 1958 'The General Line adopted on the Eighth Party Congress was studied in Peking University and publicized. CCP and government functionaries delivered reports of all sectors of the people. The city's cultural centres, bookstores, and theatres are also joining in the publicity campaign.'[21] In Tsinghua University, for example, after a series of study sessions, teachers, students, and employees passed a resolution 'that efforts should be made to make Tsinghua University, an industrial university of many departments, into an effective instrument for the proletariat in the prosecution of class struggle and production, for the purpose of satisfying the needs of the rapidly expanding industries and agriculture and meeting the needs of the technical and cultural revolution'.[22] In the middle and elementary schools, these study sessions and discussions would be confined to the administrators and the teachers. After the staff had gained a thorough understanding of the directives, they would in turn explain them to the students. This was one of the ways in which directives were transmitted to the population at large.

Since the local units had to work out concrete measures to implement the directives, there was much debate. Implementers had to come to decisions on how to allocate local resources to finance the schools, the number of schools to be built, their location, the recruitment of qualified administrators and personnel, the preparation of curricula, the allocation of land to productive labour, the recruitment of children to attend these schools, and so forth. Proceedings of meetings at which these issues were thrashed out are not available, but since one of the purposes of the mass media of China is educational, the newspapers sometimes reported to the country the difficulties faced by the advanced units and how they overcame them. From these reports, some idea of the different ideologies and outlooks and the struggles that went on can be obtained.

The training of 'red and expert' intellectuals was a subject of great debate. It was reported that: 'Some think that so long as the intellectuals perform their professional jobs well, they serve socialism. Others hold that since there is hardly time enough to become experts, it will be impossible to become both red and expert. Still others say that one who is expert and not red contributes more to the state than one who is red and not expert.'[23] The emphasis on expertise reflected the influence of the pre-liberation concept that education stood above politics. Many of the implementers were uneasy about the time devoted to ideological education and thought that the time given to productive labour would lower the quality of education.

There was considerable debate on the role of the scientists and intellectuals. The debate was particularly intense during this period when scientists were directed to go to the countryside and work alongside the peasants at local research stations. There were those who advocated that experts and intellectuals were essential in the 'real great leap forward', perhaps hinting that existing developments should not be considered as real advancements. The hegemonic ideology favoured bridging the gap between manual and mental labour but they perceived that 'scientists have large brains and small hands and are fit to invent and create, while the workers and peasants have small brains and large hands, fit only for manual labour.'[24] Statements like these were made without any evidence of recrimination at the local level, indicating that those sharing this outlook were by no means few.

Supporters of this view even challenged the leadership of the party in the educational institutions. They held that party members were usually less well educated and could not provide leadership in educational work, especially at the higher educational levels. Comments such as 'outsiders cannot lead experts', and 'men of low cultural standard cannot lead those of a higher cultural standard' were to be found in the newspapers in 1958.[25]

Non-party members were not the only ones critical of the de-emphasis on academic knowledge in education. Similar views were held by some party members. Students complaining of the heavy load of extra-curricular activities at Tsinghua University received some support from the secretary of the local Communist Party cell and president of Tsinghua who perceived ideological education as abstract: 'If everything leaps forward in the university except the students' studies, that will be too bad. We must, on the one hand, pay attention to the abstract, ideological, political work, and on the other, do our concrete work, learn our lessons well. All the lessons should be done in accordance with the teaching plan so that the abstract and the concrete may supplement each other and not be detrimental to each other.'[26] All these examples perhaps indicate that those who supported the pursuit of expertise in education were very much in a majority.

Debates on the different issues of educational development were intense and continuous. It was reported:

Whenever a practical question arises, divergent views and opinions will still arise ... when the movement of part-time labour for students was gaining momentum within the schools and educational institutions of all types and levels, some comrades expressed the fear that the movement would be a mockery of school education ... Some comrades, commenting on the increase of hours of manual labour in agricultural middle schools, thought the increase was abnormal. With regard to the development of higher education, some comrades, hearing that peasants have set up universities in the countryside would ridicule the idea, believing that a university without a staff of qualified professors and students who have graduated from senior middle schools cannot be called a university.[27]

The implementers were in general critical of the educational policy directives during this period, but because of the political dominance of the CCP, its policies had to be put into effect no matter how reluctant were some of the implementers.

IMPLEMENTATION OF THE POLICIES

The implementers did not have a high level of political consciousness; they did not completely understand the rationale behind many of the policies emanating from the centre; these they observed in form only. In the cases where the policies were more congruent with their own outlook, they carried them out with a greater degree of conscientiousness. The fidelity with which they carried out policies not to their liking would vary with the amount of pressure from the centre.

These fluctuations were exacerbated by the ways in which policies were disseminated. Directives from the centre gave only guidelines; the details had to be worked out at the local level. Different interpretations and often different strategies tailored to the local conditions resulted.

Expansion of the Educational System

The main thrust in the extension of educational facilities was in the establishment of more irregular schools, and especially the agricultural middle schools. In March, there were only two such schools in the province of Kiangsu. By June, there was an increase to 'six institutions of higher learning, 554 ordinary middle schools, 6,404 agricultural middle schools, 164 vocational middle schools, and 15,000 primary schools'.[28] This was by no means an isolated phenomenon. Over 9,000 agricultural middle schools were built in the northern provinces.

This rapid expansion in the number of schools in the rural areas was made possible by the mobilization of local resources. Intellectuals who came as a result of the anti-waste campaign provided the manpower. Peasants contributed their furniture and spare rooms to these new schools. Many experienced peasants and workers also took up teaching courses on productive skills. But this was the extent of community involvement. Local control by the masses over the educational system never materialized; this remained in the hands of the administrative cadres.

In spite of the participation of the general population, local resources were usually strained. Many of the new schools were started in great haste and were not on a firm basis:

> They were founded on short notice after some summary preparations and have since had to assume the task of fostering useful citizens with what equipment they possess. Equipment was incomplete and the teaching force inadequate. Not all the necessary cadres were provided. Either there are too many institutes or departments teaching the same subjects or there are insufficient numbers of them teaching the desired subject. All these take a toll on the quality of teaching.[29]

These weaknesses in the agricultural schools soon came to the notice of the centre. In March 1959, it was decided that some overhauling was necessary. The directives of September 1958 remained the guiding principles by which educational development was to be carried out, but minor adjustments were made throughout the period, demonstrating the dialectics of the process of policy-making and the close relationship between decision-making and the implementation of policy.

This period of expansion seems to have ended when a series of floods and droughts in mid-1959 brought worsening economic conditions, which, in turn, by late 1959, placed people's livelihood at stake; it was no longer possible for the local units to spare their manpower and financial resources to promote education. The strain imposed in financing these schools was increasingly felt. There was a blackout of news concerning the irregular schools. Later, during the Cultural Revolution, it was reported that many of them had been closed or amalgamated with regular ones nearby.

The Pursuit of Academic Quality

During this period, there were contradictory trends running through the schools. On the one hand, there was the pressure to increase the number of irregular schools. On the other hand, there was a great concern both within the party and among intellectuals generally that an increase in the number of such schools might lower their academic level when measured against that of the regular ones. Some party workers tried to 'regularize and normalize the schools' by adopting the same curriculum as the regular ones, and comparing the grades of their students with those of the latter. The attention paid to the academic quality of the irregular schools increased with the call for consolidation in March 1959. Consolidation, as put forth by the central government, meant a more rational provision of educational facilities to meet local needs. To some of the cadres at the local level, this was taken as encouragement to raise the academic standards.

There was a somewhat mechanistic approach in the implementation of educational policies; comparisons were made between the irregular and the regular schools in terms of grades achieved by the students.[30] This attitude could also be seen among the cadres of the regular schools. In response to the call for the preservation of academic standards in the directive of August 1958, the social science division of the Academy of Science reported that they hoped to finish 879 theses and fifty-one papers on Mao's work on finance, mutual aid, the cooperative movement, and the transformation of capitalism, industry, and commerce within the next five years.[31] Even within these institutes of research, academic quality was measured in terms of numbers of publications.

Another interesting feature of the implementation process was the interpretation given to the pursuit of theory and practice as embodied in Mao's thoughts. Students of Shansi and Szechwan held debates on 'For whom to study and what to study and how to study'. They proposed that 'while paying special attention to practice, systematic studies of theory should be strengthened'. Emphasis should be placed on basic courses (courses on culture). The same trend could be detected elsewhere in China:

> Institutions in other parts of the country have improved the content and methods of teaching of basic courses. Some have added new basic and theoretical courses to their curricula, and have allotted sufficient time for these courses. Full time and half day schools and primary schools, as well as sparetime schools, are also strengthening their basic courses, so that they may be adapted to the actual circumstances and both the basic

and theoretical knowledge of culture and science may be taught systematically without overemphasizing or neglecting either.[32]

In this confusing exposition on theory, practice, and 'basic' courses, it appears that the emphasis was on theory. The balance was perceived as one between culture and scientific theory, and not one between theory and practice.

Participation in Production

According to the thoughts of Mao, participation in productive labour was a way to achieve the unity of theory and practice. It was also to provide the students with an opportunity to integrate with the proletariat, to acquire the proletarian outlook, and to obtain knowledge arising from class struggle. This was the reason why labour education received such great attention during this period. For the same reason, the government placed great emphasis on the irregular schools. However, the implementers tended to see the main function of these schools as economic reconstruction. Much was made of the tangible contributions students in these schools were able to make to production:

The students of agricultural middle schools are not only good at study and labour, but are also active in social activities. They are an important force in publicizing the general line, exterminating the four evils, promoting public health, wiping out illiteracy and carrying out cultural activities. The students are good learners in school, fighters on the production front, technicians in the campaign for popularizing technology, and propaganda workers in various movements. Thus they become all-round men.[33]

The above definition of the all-round man clearly does not describe the 'red and expert' intellectuals Mao envisioned. The proletarian outlook, the socialist ideology, seem to have been forgotten here.

Though the implementers largely ignored the acquisition of the proletarian outlook, there was a closer integration of theory and practice in the agricultural schools than in the regular ones. Experienced workers and peasants were asked to teach in these schools and the subjects taught included industrial techniques and agricultural science. About a third to a half of the students' time was devoted to the practice of these techniques.

In the regular schools, the amount of productive labour required varied with the grade level of the student and his specialty. In the science universities, students generally worked in neighbouring factories or communes, in fighting insects and pests, or in the production of iron and steel. The time they spent in labour could be as long as five months per year in the higher institutes of applied science. In the social science institutes and lower down the educational scale, the time spent in productive labour was far less.

The kind of productive labour varied with the students' age and physical fitness. The work might include cleaning the school premises, planting vegetable gardens, weeding the fields, or working in the factories. The ideological aspects of labour participation were not emphasized in the implementation. All that seemed to be required by the local cadres was formal compliance to directives that often emanated as a required response to economic needs and pressure from above. As a result, during the harvest or in times of crisis, especially floods and droughts, productive labour was emphasized. At other times, the pressure from the centre was released and these programs tended to slack off.

Political Education

Political education had always been part of the curriculum since liberation, and political courses were compulsory not only at the university but also at the primary and secondary levels. However, the attention given to political courses at the local level also fluctuated with pressure from the centre. With the renewed emphasis from the centre, the courses would be taught with vigour and there would be frequent newspaper reports about them. But with the movement for consolidation and diminishing pressure from the centre in 1959, such newspaper reports became scarce, and one assumes that the enthusiasm with which these courses were taught decreased.

The way classes were conducted was most crucial in determining whether political education would raise a person's level of consciousness. Rote learning appeared to be the main vehicle of teaching in these courses, which included the study of the thoughts of Marx, Lenin, Mao, and party documents. Political education became just another academic subject. It is ironical that sometimes students with the highest marks in these courses turned out to be apolitical and conservative or were unwilling to provide their service in the remote areas where their skills were needed.

Attempts were also made to raise the teaching staff's level of political consciousness. As part of the anti-conservative campaign, debates were carried out on the question of 'red and expert' and on the dependence on western expertise. Discussions in political courses related to the analysis of current events. These discussions, however, remained at an academic level. There was no evidence of any mass campaign of criticism and self-criticism. In fact, during this period, intellectuals received special treatment; it was deliberate party policy to recruit them into the party ranks.

OUTCOME OF EDUCATIONAL DEVELOPMENT

As the foregoing shows, educational development was the result of a complex process of interaction between the ideology of the different policy-makers, their perception of the objective reality, and the support the different opinions could muster. In turn, local conditions influenced the ways in which policies were implemented. Within the limits of the direction pointed out by the centre, the way in which a policy was implemented was affected by the ideology of the implementers, their power alignments, fluctuating pressure from the centre, and local economic and social conditions. The outcome of the educational policies of the GLF was the result of a combination of all these factors.

In fact, the outcome of the GLF policies fell far short of the goals set out in the directive. The Maoist goals had been to universalize education, to close the gap between rural and urban areas, to integrate theoretical knowledge with practical considerations, and to instil the proletarian outlook generally. To a large extent, the implementers subverted the achievement of these goals by emphasizing the technological and the economic aspects of education and by undermining the more radical policies by a formalistic presentation. This, together with the capitalist tendencies in the

Table 11   Student Enrolment 1958–59
(Numbers in Thousands)

Year	Higher Education	Secondary Technical	Secondary General	Primary
1957	441	780	6,280	64,280
1958	660	1,470	8,520	86,400
1959	810		12	90,000

Source: Ten Great Years (Peking: Foreign Languages Press, 1960), p. 192, and Jan S. Prybyla, The Political Economy of Communist China (Scranton: International Textbook Co., 1970), p. 449.

economic base and local objective conditions, affected the successful implementation of the policies.

However, despite these obstacles, the universalizing of education met with reasonable success, especially if educational development is measured in terms of the increase in enrolment. According to official statistics, in 1958, enrolment in primary schools increased by 34 percent, in secondary schools by 70 percent, and in universities by 50 percent. These figures might be a little exaggerated, but they are not entirely improbable.[34]

The bulk of the increase came from the irregular schools. One source estimated that out of the increase of 24 million students enrolled in schools in 1958, 22 million were attending irregular schools.[35] This might be an overestimation, but there is no doubt that the increase in enrolment was spectacular, especially at the secondary and higher levels where it was easier to set up work/study schools. Students at these levels were physically more equipped to perform productive labour and in a better position to help the schools to attain self-sufficiency. This increase might also be related to the deficiency existing at the secondary level in 1958. In the years immediately after liberation, there was a tremendous increase in the enrolment in primary schools, but only one in ten of these graduates went on to attend secondary school. Though such a rationale was not articulated by the central gov-

Table 12   Enrolment in Part-Time and Spare-Time Schools
(Numbers in Thousands)

Year	University	Secondary	Junior Secondary	Literacy Class
1957	7.6	271.4	627.7	720.8
1958	15	500	2,600	4,000
1959	30	500	738	2,440

Source: *New China Yearbook* 1965, p. 384.

ernment, the attempt to increase enrolment in this direction might have been a pragmatic decision to create a larger pool of educated workers.

Achievement was also spectacular in the redistribution of educational opportunity. While statistics are incomplete and there would be much variation throughout the country, great advances were undoubtedly made, especially in rural areas and the more remote regions. In the autonomous areas of Tibet and Mongolia, the increase in enrolment was as great as 50 percent. In Anhwei, enrolment of children in primary schools increased from 48 percent to 92 percent at the end of 1958; and in some hsien (counties) and cities they achieved universal primary education. Primary attendance over the country was estimated to be 85 percent in 1959.[36]

There was also a major redistribution of educational opportunities in terms of class background. The greatest effort was made in the rural areas, where the beneficiaries were mostly peasants, who could not afford to send their children to the regular schools. Now they could send their sons and daughters to schools in the neighbourhood. These schools were cheaper, their children could earn work points (a system by which income was distributed in the communes) while attending school, and they could retain the labour power of their children during the busy season. Statistics on students from a peasant background are not available, but data show that the average annual rate of increase of students from peasant worker background between 1949–57 was about 2 percent; in 1958 the rate was 10 percent.[37]

Table 13 Percentage of Students from Worker-Peasant Class

Year	University	Vocational Secondary	General Secondary
1957	36.3	66.6	69.1
1958	49.0	77.0	75.2

Source: *New China Yearbook* 1965, p. 385.

It might be noted, however, that the sex ratio of the students remained relatively stable with more boys than girls enrolled at all levels.[38] This may be because a large number of male children were without education but it seems more likely, in view of the traditional preferential treatment for male children, that efforts to increase enrolment still accrued to the boys. It was only in the sixties that this situation changed and a gradual increase in female student population could be detected.

One of the major aims of the educational policy of the GLF was to raise the level of consciousness of the younger generation. The success in this direction is hard to evaluate, but attempts had been made to raise their political consciousness. The participation of students in labour was a first attempt to break the traditional concept that the intellectuals worked with their brains alone. The establishment of the irregular schools, especially the agricultural work/study schools, was an eye-opener for both the cadres and the masses; it exposed them to an alternative mode of education. Education, in their eyes, used to mean nice looking classrooms, with complete sets of equipment and apparatus, libraries, and western-trained professors. The irregular schools presented an alternative and more flexible model, with makeshift provisions and teaching personnel from all walks of life. They also presented education not as a channel to becoming a government official but to improving services in their own localities through their own production. Through their efforts to install these schools, the masses gradually became more aware of their own potential. They found that they could not only build irrigation canals and open agricultural lands; they could also build and run their own schools.

Another achievement was a technical one—the contribution to regional economic development. Students were sent to the surrounding rural areas or factories to help in production, and their presence helped to bolster the morale of the workers and accomplish some labour-intensive projects. It was reported that 1,700,000 youths helped to complete over 33,400 medium and small-scale irrigation projects. Similar numbers of students in Hopei extended the farming acreage by three million mou. Research institutes set up in the local areas helped to disseminate new agricultural techniques, solve local agricultural problems, exterminate pests, and increase production.[39] Without the presence of these trained personnel, these projects could probably not have been carried out.

We have concentrated on the accomplishments of the policies of the GLF and the extent to which they were implemented and proved successful. In the next chapter, we examine why, in spite of these apparent successes, a change of policy occurred in 1960.

The Period of Retrenchment: 1960–1962

Despite the apparent success of the policies of the GLF in helping to equalize the distribution of educational opportunities in China and to bridge the gap between manual and mental labour, urban and rural areas, they were nevertheless abandoned and replaced.

ABANDONMENT OF THE POLICIES OF THE GLF

The GLF had called for a greater rate of growth in the economy as well as in education and for the simultaneous development of industry and agriculture. Sideline industries were to be set up in the countryside. These policies were initially undertaken with great enthusiasm. In Anhua, for example, it was reported that 2,100 factories were set up within a few months. The Red Scarf Reservoir, which irrigated 200 mou of land, was completed in one day with 780 men working at it. However, the lack of planning and the haste with which these projects were carried out resulted in many not being up to standard.[1] For example, some of the reservoir and irrigation canals dried up in the drought season, and much of the steel produced in home foundries was not good enough for industrial use.

The result was a great waste of resources and, in addition, a considerable diversion of manpower from agriculture. In some areas, the manpower devoted to new projects was well over 80 percent. In a village that one observer visited, most of the able-bodied had been transferred to a nearby irrigation project. Only 130 out of the 780 workers were left behind to save the harvest on the eve of an impending storm.[2] Thus, instead of supporting agriculture, such attempts undermined its growth.

The communes also became plagued by an unwarranted spirit of competition. When they first started, the aim had been distribution according to needs. In practice, distribution continued to be made according to labour contributed; only certain items were allocated according to need. Communes vied with each other on the number of these items to be distributed free to their members. The list of free supplies sometimes extended beyond their means, often because the cadres responsible overestimated the capacity of the communes. Moreover, having contracted with the state to meet quotas, they subsequently were unable to fulfil them. In some cases, they even contracted to produce certain crops with which the members of the communes had no previous experience. These two factors frequently combined to result in an actual lowering of production.

All this might eventually have righted itself had it not been for natural disasters. In early 1959, there were serious floods in southern China, while in the north there was a period of prolonged drought. In that year, about 100 million acres, probably amounting to half of the arable land, were suffering from either drought or flood. And in 1960, the areas affected by natural disasters increased: '[A] combination of drought, typhoons, floods, and pests struck 150 million acres, more than half of the crop lands, and seriously affected 50–60 million acres, which had no crops at all. Nor were the difficulties over; drought still continued through the winter of 1960–61 in the northern wheatlands, only slightly relieved by two snowfalls prior to the drought.'[3] These natural disasters affected not only agriculture but the output of light and heavy industry, which depended on agriculture for their supply of raw material.

Faced with the deteriorating conditions, emergency measures were taken in 1959. Students and city workers were exhorted to help in crop production and harvesting; local manpower was enlisted. The work/study schools, which were largely dependent on local support, were depleted. Later, during the Cultural Revolution, it was revealed that, in the early sixties, many irregular schools had been closed down or amalgamated with neighbouring regular schools. With the very livelihood of people at stake, education inevitably suffered.

The future of the work/study schools was affected by changes in the level of production as well as by the survival of many capitalist characteristics in the social relations of production. Rewards were still distributed not according to need but according to one's position in a hierarchy and based on academic attainment. Graduates of the regular schools had greater access to comparatively well-paid government jobs in the cities. Little wonder, then, that most of the masses and the implementers of the GLF policies saw the graduates of the irregular schools as being 'condemned' to life in the countryside. As long as this system of differential rewards continued, people would continue to reject the agricultural schools, the lower stream of the two-track educational system, which frustrated their hopes of acquiring high positions in the new socialist order.

The educational system was also more susceptible to economic influences through its own inherent contradictions. The lingering capitalist characteristics here were even more strongly entrenched than in the economy. The educated were highly respected; the involvement of the less educated masses in school administration was viewed by many as illegitimate. Rote remained the dominant mode of learning within the schools, rendering political studies just another abstract, theoretical subject. The competitive examination and grading system, which rewarded one's ability to regurgitate memorized material, further reinforced this academic trend. The rules of conduct for students, which called for respect of authority, politeness, and good behaviour, bound the students still closer to acceptance of the existing system. In a climate which emphasized individual and academic achievement, attempts to mobilize the masses and to integrate theory with practice, 'redness and expertise', could never be wholly successful.

The educational policies of the GLF probably would not have been abandoned so completely had the lack of immediate success in implementing ideological education or mass mobilization been the only factor working against them. The policies, especially at the implementation level, were abandoned because they ran counter to the entrenched view that maintaining high academic standards was the mandate of educational institutes. Many still perceived the educational system mainly as a transmitter of knowledge. True, the academic and technological aspects of education were emphasized at this time. But, with continuing pressure from the centre to expand educational facilities, particularly those for ideological education, the implementers increased the time students were to spend in production, both to express compliance with official guidelines and to ensure another source of financing for the new schools. The result was a proliferation of a large number of schools, accompanied by a lowering of academic standards. This further convinced the implementers of the inappropriateness of the educational policies of the GLF. When the opportunity arose, they were ready to do away with the irregular schools. Educational development. thus, was shaped as much by its own internal dynamics as by the economy.

SHIFTING ALLIANCES AT THE CENTRE

The alacrity with which the work/study schools were closed was also an indication of the decline in support from the centre. The outcome of the policies of the GLF forced the departments concerned to reconsider their policies. A shift in position at the centre was detectable as early as December 1958. Following the call for the establishment of the communes in August 1958, many cadres at the local level exceeded their instructions and confiscated private plots as well as sideline industries and chattels. Fear of confiscation led many peasants to slaughter their livestock. Also, no provision had been made for the collective pursuit of domestic handicrafts and sideline industries. The result was severe economic dislocation; shortages of pigs, poultry, vegetables, and such implements as brooms for both urban and rural use.

As these shortcomings in the GLF policy became increasingly visible, Mao resigned. When he announced his resignation as chairman of the State in December 1958, the reason given was that he wished 'to concentrate his energies on dealing with the questions of direction, policy, and the line of the party and the state, ... to set aside more time for Marxist-Leninist study'.[4]

Whether his resignation was forced on him or was voluntary is beside the point. But some changes in the balance of power had probably occurred, since his resignation was also accompanied by shifts in policy. Soon after, the central government denounced the wholesale confiscation of personal property and brought forward the resolution that all private means of livelihood, together with bank credit, deposits, tools, and fruit trees, were to remain in private ownership, in perpetuity. In January 1959, *Red Flag*, the party journal, stated that peasants should be allowed to grow vegetables around their houses. Private raising of pigs was encouraged. Then in March 1959, came the call to consolidate the existing schools that had been set up in the provinces.[5]

These policy shifts do not necessarily mean that there was a rejection of the principles enunciated by Mao during the GLF. They could mean that, given the general level of political consciousness and existing economic conditions, the policies of the GLF were recognized as premature. Consolidation, with a slower rate of growth and more coordinated planning, was necessary. Even Mao realized that there were weaknesses. In July, at a meeting in Lushan, he admitted that he had underestimated the scale and complexity of the situation: 'Coal and iron will not walk by themselves and had to be transported by rolling stock. ... I did not anticipate this point'.[6]

The meeting at Lushan, in July 1959, gave perhaps the clearest indication that there was indeed a power struggle and conflict within the ruling group. At this meeting, Mao's policy of the GLF came under direct attack. P'eng Te-huai, head of the People's Liberation Army (PLA), characterized the policies of 1958 as 'petty bourgeois fanaticism'. The crucial issue seemed to centre around the differing emphases Mao and P'eng put on social activism: 'In the view of some comrades, putting politics in command could be a substitute for everything. Putting politics in command is not a substitute for economic principles, still less for the concrete measures in economic work. Equal importance must be attached to putting politics in command and the effective measures in economic work.'[7] P'eng's point was that unless the forces of production were mechanized and the level of production raised, it would be impossible to transform Chinese society into a socialist one.

It seems unlikely that P'eng would have launched such an obvious attack on the policies of Mao without what he estimated to be adequate support. But if this was the case, P'eng guessed wrong. He was dismissed from his position, and others in the PLA were demoted. Judging from those who were affected, it appears that he had considerable support in the provinces of Hunan, Shantung, and Kansu, but not enough for him to keep his position of power.[8]

Later, during the Cultural Revolution, it was alleged that Liu Shao-ch'i had supported P'eng in 1959. This may have been true in 1962, when Liu did ask for the review of P'eng's case, but it does not necessarily mean that he had supported P'eng at this particular juncture. It could be argued, of course, that although it was Liu who announced P'eng's dismissal in 1959, he had, nevertheless, supported P'eng behind the scenes. Unlike Lin Piao, however, conspiracy did not appear to be one of Liu's weaknesses; even his accusers during the Cultural Revolution regarded his record as 'clean' in 1958 and 1959.[9] A more plausible interpretation put forward by Dittmer holds that Liu represented the moderate between the two extremes (Mao and P'eng) on this occasion.[10] But in view of the fact that a person's opinion is subject to modification in light of changing conditions, and the lack of concrete evidence that Liu had supported P'eng, it seems more likely that Liu sided with Mao in 1959 and only came into conflict with him later.

It may be that the Maoist group were united in their opposition to the rightist position of P'eng until the beginning of 1960. The economic situation continued to deteriorate, in spite of several adjustments made in the previous year. Added to this, the Russians withdrew their aid at this time. Over a thousand Russian experts working in China were recalled and took with them their blueprints. Many of the projects started with their help were left unfinished. With this sudden withdrawal, China was left on her own. Perhaps at this stage, Liu and others began to question the suitability of the GLF policies in China's socialist reconstruction, which demonstrates the role of objective reality in shaping outlook as well as development.

However, all the individuals involved did not react in like manner to the changing conditions. Liu's opposition to Mao on the question of the role of technology and coordination in socialist reconstruction was supported by the majority of the party and government leaders, including Lu Ting-i, T'ao Chu, and Chou Yang. Most of them had been educated in foreign countries or in universities run by foreign missionaries, and in view of their background, it might be expected that they would opt for development through industrialization and dependence on experts.

Mao, however, because of his faith in man's ability to change his environment, reacted differently. In April 1960, he published his article 'On Contradictions' written in 1937, in which he stated that: 'True, the productive forces, practice, and the economic base generally play the principal and decisive role; whoever denies this is not materialist. But it must also be admitted that under certain conditions, such aspects as the relations of production, theory, and the superstructure, in turn manifest themselves in the principal and decisive role.'[11] In publishing this article in the *People's Daily*, Mao may have been using the mass media to publicize his point. It may also be an indication that he could not summon enough support within the hegemonic group and so turned to the people. He asserted that a more active attempt should be made to transform the ideology of the masses so that the complete socialist transformation of the economy could take place. One could not rely on the forces of production alone. Nonetheless, the majority did not fully realize the dangers inherent in relying exclusively on technical experts to raise China's level of production, and his strategy, it appears, did not gain enough support at the time.

In the same year, the play *Dismissal of Hai Jui from Office* was published. Like many stories and plays written during that period, it lauded the role of kings, ministers, princes, and generals of the feudal era and played down the role of the common people. Later, during the Cultural Revolution, this play was singled out for attack because it was also an oblique reference to the case of P'eng, in which the emperor (Mao) would not listen to the righteous advice of his minister (P'eng). The fact that it could be published and its writer, Wu Han, remain unchallenged until the mid-sixties, shows that Mao's position had been much weakened with the debacle of the GLF.

With the different reactions to the economic conditions and the shifts in the power balance within the hegemonic group, there were accompanying shifts in the policies of the GLF that finally culminated in a major policy change, which went beyond mere readjustment and consolidation. The policies of the GLF were reaffirmed after P'eng's dismissal in 1959, but in practice there was a decided departure from them between 1960 and 1962, a time known as the Period of Retrenchment.

POLICIES OF THE PERIOD OF RETRENCHMENT

In the draft plan for 1960, announced at the Second Session of the Second People's Congress, Li Fu-chun, the vice premier, reaffirmed the policies of the GLF:

The national economic development task in 1960 is to better carry out the Party's general line, building socialism and to strive for a continued, all round, and better leap forward in the national economy on the basis of the last two years' continuous leap forward.

He continued:

The arrangement of the 1960 national economic plan must further confirm agriculture as the foundation, and industry as the leading factor; combine priority of heavy industry with rapid development of agriculture; continue the policy of making overall arrangements, with steel as the key factor in industry and grain as the key lever in agriculture; and further strengthen transport, the extraction as well as the mining industry, so as to handle more appropriately the balance between heavy industry, light industry, and agriculture, as well as those different trades and branches within those departments, and achieve a better leap forward in the national economy.[12]

The National Program for Agricultural Development was adopted at the same congress.

When the conditions in agriculture did not recover quickly despite the increasing emphasis put on agriculture, all sectors of the population in 1962 were called upon to help: 'The congress calls upon the people of all nationalities and departments of industry, agriculture, communication, finance, banking, trade, science, education, culture, public health, and physical culture to exert concerted effort in the struggle for the realization of the national agricultural program two or three years ahead of schedule.'[13] As for industry and commerce, they were exhorted to support agriculture:

In the field of industry, the first thing to do, in accordance with the needs of the technical transformation of agriculture and the present availability of materials and manpower, is to carry out further the rational re-adjustment [and] strengthen the productive capability of the weaker department. ... In the field of commerce, it is necessary, in accordance with the principle of insuring supplies by increasing production, and the policy of serving agriculture and industrial production and the livelihood of the people, and through the channels of state-run commerce, cooperative commerce, and village trade fairs, to make greater efforts to arrange for the interflow of farm produce and manufactured goods between the rural and urban areas, so as to supply them with more means of production, supply industries with more materials, and supply the urban and rural people with more daily necessities.[14]

This change in emphasis on the relative importance of industry and agriculture was, in fact, a significant departure from the policies of the GLF, which had called for the simultaneous growth of the two sectors.

As a remedy for the haphazard manner in which policies were implemented during the GLF, the hegemonic group, during this period, emphasized coordination and planning. The country was a great 'chessboard'; development in one area would have repercussions on another. The success of the whole depended on the successes of its parts. According to this rationale, careful central planning was essential: 'There must be unified policies, plans, and systems for carrying out the unified allocation of manpower and material supplies and financial resources within a certain compass, so as to ensure the development of the national economy in a planned manner, proportionately and at high speed.'[15] Greater attention was to be paid to the implementation process at the lower levels. The cadres were advised

to carry out correctly the policies of the party and the State. The leadership at different levels and the different enterprises must, within the compass of their own powers and rights, conscientiously study the concrete circumstances to find out effective measures based upon finding truth from facts. In order to bring the different tasks laid down in state plans to realization, they must also create all kinds of favourable conditions by all means, and fully depend on the strength and wisdom of the masses.[16]

The call to study local conditions carefully was a measure intended to remedy the unrealistic targets and bloated statistics on achievements sent to the centre during the GLF. At the Second Session of the Eighth National Party Congress, Liu Shao-ch'i warned that the cadres should not 'indulge in empty talk or bluff'. The targets put forward should be achievable through hard work. The cadres should not publicize unrealistic plans.

Great emphasis was also put on technological advancement. Tan Chen-lin, speaking on the Program for Agricultural Development in April 1960, reported that 'a movement for technical innovation and technical revolution centring on mechanization or semi-mechanization and automation or semi-automation'[17] was underway in all departments throughout the country.

While the GLF had also emphasized the importance of technological advances to aid development in the late fifties, exclusive emphasis was now placed on technology and planning, with little or no attention to mass line, mass mobilization, or mass initiative. Further, Liu Shao-ch'i announced in 1961 that technological experimentation was to be carried out solely at the provincial level; this statement is not entirely unexpected, given the emphasis he put on objective feasibility. A centralized system of experimentation would be more efficient. By the end of the year, only ninety-two local research centres remained out of the hundreds created during the GLF.[18]

Material incentives were now used to mobilize the masses. No official statements condoning this practice can be found, probably because such inducements are a negation of the communist ideology. Rather, it took place with passive official connivance.[19] In 1961, it was stipulated that peasants could keep private plots on a long-term basis, not exceeding 5 percent of the collective acreage. With regard to sideline industries:

> The relevant documents on the rural peoples' commune state that, provided the growth of the collective economy is not impeded and the absolute dominance of the collective economy is ensured, the peoples' commune should permit and encourage members to carry on sideline occupations during leisure hours and on off days. Within the scope of family sideline industries, members are permitted to tend a small amount of private plots and open up odd plots of wasteland.[20]

On the surface, in both the late fifties and the early sixties, the government encouraged sideline industries in the rural areas.

But the nature of these sideline industries had changed. In the late fifties, they were run on a communal basis to support agricultural development. In the early sixties, they were carried out as individual or family projects to increase private income and the supply of goods circulating in the country.

At the beginning of 1960, payment in the communes was according to work performed, supplemented by free supplies. In the cities, payment was on the basis of time spent on the job. By 1962, payment of wages was generally on a piece rate in both rural and urban areas, with special rewards being paid to those who exceeded their quota. The labour market became increasingly one with a graduated scale of pecuniary rewards. These policies to motivate the individual through material gains were epitomized in the catch phrase 'Three Selfs and One Guarantee' (san tzu i pao) which refers to the 'extension of plots for private use, the rural free market, increase of small enterprises responsible for their own profits and losses' and 'fixing of output quotas based on the individual households'.[21] Such deviations from the policy of the GLF did not go unopposed. In 1962, there was a proliferation of articles defending the use of piece rates and profit as a gauge of efficiency, perhaps indicating growing opposition from the Maoist group.

EDUCATIONAL POLICY:
A REFLECTION OF THE ECONOMIC POLICY

The changes in educational policy bore a great resemblance to those on the economic front. Changes in both sectors were needed to correct the weaknesses in the policy of the GLF. The rationalizations for these changes were couched within the framework of the accepted official ideology. There was a reaffirmation of the policy of the GLF, but underlying it were major departures from its basic principles.

In April 1960, Yang Hsiao-feng, the minister of education, announced that:

> To develop education, we must adhere firmly to the educational policy of the Party, the policy of coordinating the work of extending university education to all persons, with the task of raising the standards of education, the policy of walking on

two legs, and the policy of developing higher education and middle schools education, speeding up the universalization of the elementary school education, and enormously developing spare-time education among the workers and peasants.[22]

Accompanying the growing emphasis on agriculture in the economy was a comparable emphasis on the supportive role of education in agricultural development: 'Educational institutions should take up the work of supporting agriculture as their glorious task. More schools to serve the interest of local production and construction should be established.'[23] From announcements like these, it may appear that the policies of the GLF were still closely adhered to, namely, the development of education through both regular and irregular schools. The central purpose of education still seemed to be to serve local production and construction. However, rhetoric notwithstanding, the emphasis now was radically different from that pursued by the GLF, and there were basic differences in the strategies of the dominant factions during this period.

Instead of emphasizing the role of mass mobilization in transforming China's economic base and superstructure, the dominant faction in the early sixties stressed the adaptation to objective conditions. By their reasoning, the growth and extension of facilities was circumscribed by the prevailing economic circumstances. Expansion should be confined to the spare-time schools; it could not be extended to the work/study schools. In 1960, Lu Ting-i elaborated this point: 'Limited by the economic conditions of the peoples' commune and due to the fact that there is still a manpower shortage in agriculture, any number of spare-time senior middle schools may be established, but it is impossible to set up many half-day senior middle schools at present. However, the number will certainly gradually increase.'[24]

Members of the dominant faction also had a different conception of the purpose of education, which they considered to be the raising of the level of technological development of the country. They perceived the schools as centres that disseminate a high level of culture and technical knowledge and were disturbed at the lowering of academic standards that occurred during the GLF. In expressing this viewpoint, Lu said: 'Although much progress has been made in middle and elementary school education in general, cultural standards have been lowered in some respects, as exemplified by the elimination of analytical geometry from the curricula of senior middle schools and the adoption of lower standards in foreign languages.' As a result of these considerations, he suggested that:

> If only we can properly reform our teaching methods, revise our textbooks, strengthen the leadership of the CCP committees attached to the schools, and organize large scale coordinated cooperation between teachers to change their present practice of each tending his own business without coordination, it will be quite possible for us suitably to shorten the number of school years, raise the educational standards, tighten control over study hours, and increase physical labour.[25]

Citing numerous experiments that had been carried out in the various schools to improve teaching techniques, he further cautioned: 'We are not in a hurry to issue decrees governing the new schooling system to be adopted throughout the country. Even in the future, when the new schooling system is adopted, a period will be granted for the people to implement it on a trial basis.'[26] In essence, Lu was opting for improvements in the educational system that would raise the general academic level. Education for ideological transformation was completely ignored. Until his academic targets were reached, he warned, it would be difficult to shorten time spent in schooling or increase the time given to physical labour.

His caution was perhaps warranted, given the impatience with which policies had been implemented during the GLF. But his policy went beyond consolidation in education; it was a change in policy. The call for the expansion of spare-time schools and improving academic quality was geared to the increasing demand for a high level of technology and skilled manpower in the changing model of economic development.

The two announcements of Yang and Lu were made about the same time, yet they had different emphases, reflecting perhaps conflict of opinions among the decision-makers. The policy promulgated by Lu Ting-i, which emphasized the importance of technology rather than ideology, dominated in the next two years. Wang Jang-chung said that one should learn from old farmers, even though they might be conservative in outlook. Ch'en Yi was quoted as saying that professional schools should concentrate on professional training.[27] However, there were dangers in the dominant policy. What was overlooked was the possibility that a disproportionate emphasis on technology in socialist reconstruction could lead to the growth of a new elite based on technical skills and reinforce the capitalist tendencies already existent in the educational system.

IMPLEMENTATION OF THE NEW EDUCATIONAL POLICIES

If there was opposition to the new emphasis on raising academic levels in the schools, the voices were not strong enough to be heard. The only oblique indication of some kind of dissatisfaction at the implementation level came from letters to the newspapers, in which peasants expressed their support for the people-run schools (mostly work/study schools). Many of the peasants had boycotted these schools at their inception in 1958 because they did not coincide with their traditional perception of schools, but by 1960, they had begun to appreciate their role in training rural young people in reading, writing, and accounting. Their letters indicated regret that many of these schools had been closed.[28]

In general, the response to the educational policies of 1960 to 1962 was one of acceptance, if not enthusiasm. This can be seen in the newspaper coverage of the subject. In the years 1958–59, there had been newspaper reports on problems encountered, and discussion sessions were held to convince the implementers of the advantages of unity of theory and practice, 'redness and expertise'. In the early sixties, there were no reports of such discussions. It might be argued that, in the general atmosphere of centralization, discussion at the grassroots level, which characterized the GLF, had been cut short. However, the reversed administrative approach did not prevent discussions on the utility of material incentives, or on the retention of rural markets and private property, reflecting an uneasiness that these measures might be considered as deviations from the socialist line. It may be that there was no debate on the subject of raising academic levels because, even to many in the ruling group at this particular point, there was no direct or obvious relationship between the raising of academic levels and the growth of capitalist characteristics. The implementers of these educational policies required no rationalization to convince them of the advantages of doing academic research or raising academic levels. In fact, the directives from the centre were carried out with much enthusiasm. The number of courses was increased, the curriculum was revised, the hours devoted to productive labour were reduced, and special attention was paid to academic research. The universities were especially active in these reforms.

Raising Academic Standards

A number of measures were used to raise academic standards. The curriculum was revamped and new courses were added, especially at the university level where the professors had a free hand in organizing them. Outdated material was discarded and up-to-date courses in the sciences were included. There was also an increasing emphasis on specialization; for example, courses on rural banking and commodity circulation were added, and at Peking University, even new courses disseminating bourgeois ideology were offered: 'When subjects of idealism and academic thoughts of the bourgeoisie were taught and introduced, the teachers usually gave an all-round introduction to the subjects in the first instance, and whether such subjects were critically taught was for the teachers themselves to decide.'[29] The offering of such courses was considered to be in line with the party's guideline of 'letting a hundred flowers bloom and diverse schools of thought contend.'

In an attempt to improve the quality of teaching, team teaching and collective efforts were encouraged among the staff. Experienced professors and teachers were given special responsibilities. They were asked to head groups of young teachers, supervise preparation of lesson plans, and train teachers in the field. To ensure that adequate time would be devoted to class preparation and teaching, teachers in the middle schools were to devote no less than three units of their time per week (morning, afternoon, and evening were each considered a unit) to meetings.

Particular efforts were made to train 'advanced' students, that is, those who had high academic standing. Special arrangements were made to give them extra guidance and special assignments. The aim, it was stated, was not only to help these pioneering talents, but to encourage others to compete with them.[30] This encouragement of competition was in conflict, not only with the socialist ideal of cooperation, but, in the special treatment accorded to the more academically gifted, with the socialist ideal of training 'red and expert' intellectuals.

Teaching aids mainly in the form of educational hardware were provided to facilitate teaching. In the middle schools of Nanking: 'Teachers of natural sciences were required to strengthen the link between theory and practice, to produce teaching aids energetically, and to use electrical devices for teaching. Tape recorders were used for teaching foreign languages, slides were used for the teaching of botany.'[31] With the emphasis now on the adoption of expensive innovations, it is unlikely that, given the economic conditions in China, all the schools would be provided with such facilities. More probably, they were confined to a few regular schools. It is ironic that the employment of teaching aids was justified on the grounds of the unity of theory and practice, since the meaning attached to the word 'practice' was contrary to that used by Mao.

New equipment was also installed at the research institutes and universities to ensure that scientists could carry on their experiments. Tsinghua University, for example, reported that 'the number of laboratories increased from 50 in 1957 to 81 at present. The original equipment in the laboratories has all been reinforced and improved. In certain respects, the university has acquired production techniques enabling us to make relatively intricate laboratory equipment'.[32] New provisions were made to ensure that scientists could devote their energy to research. In some universities, it was stipulated that no less than five-sixths of their time should be devoted to academic pursuits. Large numbers of conferences were also held to encourage academic exchange, the topics ranging from economic theories to psychology, genetics to polymer chemistry. Papers presented and discussed during these meetings appeared to be mostly theoretical. A discussion on art and literature, for example, stressed literary techniques and professionalism, classical Chinese, and foreign art. No attempt was made to relate theories to practical realities.

Ideological Education
Ideological education was still considered important in principle. In practice, however, integration with workers and peasants and

the acquisition of the proletarian outlook was seldom mentioned. In a teacher's college 'those who have not finished the three political courses are required to attend supplementary classes according to plan. Those who have already finished the three political courses are to attend special lectures on Marxism-Leninism and Mao Tse-tung's classical works, so that their knowledge in theory may be raised.'[33] Ideological education was measured in terms of the number of courses taken in political theory. The mechanistic approach pursued during the GLF was still to be found.

Participation in labour to acquire a proletarian outlook is seldom mentioned in reports of the period. Instead, the official line emphasized adequate rest; there was no time set aside for participation in labour or political education. In the schedule for school students, primary students were to spend nine to ten hours a day relaxing, middle school students eight to nine hours, and university students not less than eight hours. In the city of Tientsin, some schools made provisions for afternoon naps, which sometimes lasted as long as seventy minutes. The number and length of meetings were cut down. In Tsinghua University, the students were to have seven hours of rest, social activities, and physical training, eight hours of sleep, and nine hours of study.[34]

In early 1960, there were some reports of students and teachers helping in the 'work of the three autumns' (harvesting, ploughing, and sowing). In the next two years, such reports disappeared. Some students did go to the rural areas to learn to relate theory and practice through work, but their numbers remained small. Even when they did so, their main aim was to carry out studies and surveys of local conditions and to relate their findings to the theories they learned in the classroom. Chungshang Medical School helped the communes to improve sanitation and train health personnel. South China Agricultural College helped to work out innovations in agriculture and carried out research on the soil. Kwangtung Hydro-Electric Power College surveyed and designed irrigation and water conservation projects.[35] These activities may well have been beneficial to the people living in the rural areas, but the ideological aspect of working with the peasants was neglected.

However, there was increasing attention paid to extra-curricular activities, and growing recognition of the role of society in socializing the young. It was recognized that parents play a decisive role in bringing up the young, and they were exhorted to encourage their children to read enlightening books, or to prepare them to accept work assignments after graduation.

Much research was done on children's reading materials and games at this time. These studies revealed that many in current use had detrimental effects on the ideology of the younger generation. In consequence, after-school activities were expanded and children were organized into groups that played and worked together after school, under the supervision of tutors, while their parents were still at work. Neighbourhood children's libraries were also opened. Within the schools, the Communist Youth League and the Young Pioneers became more active; however, one of their major functions was still to help backward students in their studies. These organizations, in addition, arranged visits to promote class education; for example, students went to rural areas and factories to listen to peasants and workers recounting their past experiences under the KMT government. One might also mention the 'Three Good Youth Movement', which was launched to promote good health, good morals, and good academic standards among the students.

Expansion of the Educational System
The targets for increased enrolment, published in 1960, anticipated an increase of 280,000 in higher education, 600,000 in specialized secondary schools, 800,000 in senior secondary schools, 4 million in junior secondary schools, and 2.8 million in vocational and other agricultural schools. The increase was mainly at the university and high school levels.[36] The primary school target was left off the list. This perhaps reflected the government's bias on training experts.

No further statistics were released in the following two years, making it impossible to gauge the expansion of education during this period. It appears that, true to the official guideline, expansion occurred mainly within the spare-time schools in the industrial towns of Shenyang, Shanghai, and Tientsin. Financial enterprises, factories, government departments, and institutes of higher learning were the main sponsors. Workers enrolled in these schools spent six to eight hours a week in study. In Shanghai, about 1.8 million workers were enrolled in 8,700 spare-time schools. In Shengyang, seven out of every ten workers were in school. Graduates sent to the countryside were also encouraged to enrol in spare-time schools. However, because of the lack of adequate facilities, it appears that the number of these schools was small.[37]

The policies during this period seem to have been congruent with the ideology of the implementers for they received little opposition and required little or no persuasion. However, this did not mean that the desired results—that is, education for the socialist reconstruction of China—were achieved. The main result was to reinforce the growing capitalist tendencies in Chinese society and retard the development of socialist ones.

OUTCOME OF EDUCATIONAL DEVELOPMENT:
AN EVALUATION

What was the outcome of educational development during this period? To what extent were the aims of the hegemonic group fulfilled?

It must be pointed out here that even though the emphasis at this time was on consolidation and the raising of academic levels, the ultimate aim was still socialist reconstruction. The effect of the policy shift, however, was to slow down social change. There was an overall drop in enrolment during this period; enrolment in the universities rose 17.9 percent over the previous year in 1960, but dropped about 14 percent in the next two years. At the secondary level, it increased by 16 percent in 1960, dropped by 13 percent in 1961, and by 8 percent in 1962. At the primary level, there was a steady drop over the three year period at the rate of 6 percent, 11 percent, and 4 percent respectively. The general rate of decline might be attributed to deteriorating economic conditions, but the greater rate of decline at the secondary and primary levels was the result of deliberate official policies to close down the work/study schools. The only area where some increase occurred was in the spare-time schools; however, these increases were mainly confined to a few industrial cities and were by no means widespread.

The poorest sector of society was the hardest hit by this shrinkage in educational opportunities. Ten years after liberation, inequality was still present in Chinese society. Differences between the rich and the poor could still be found, and standards of

Table 14 Student Enrolment in China 1960–63 (Numbers in Thousands)

School Year	Higher Education		Middle Schools		Primary Schools	
	Number	Percentage Difference*	Number	Percentage Difference	Number	Percentage Difference
1959–60	810		12,900		90,000	
1960–61	955	+17.90	15,000	+16.57	85,000	– 5.56
1961–62	819	–14.24	13,100	–12.67	76,000	–10.59
1962–63	820	+ 0.12	12,000	– 8.40	73,000	– 3.95

Source: Jan S. Prybyla, *The Political Economy of Communist China* (Scranton: International Textbook Company, 1970), p. 449.

* Percentages are calculated over total of the previous year.

living were higher in the urban than in the rural areas. With the closing of the irregular schools, the proletariat, and especially the poor peasants, were excluded from education. A student required 108 yuan annually to attend regular school, but only 38 yuan for a work/study one. When the average monthly wage in China was about 70 yuan, it would be difficult for a worker to provide regular education for all his children.[38] Since most of the work/study schools were located in the rural areas, their closing was the peasants' loss.

The open system of education was now replaced by an elitist one. Not only were educational opportunities fewer, but strong emphasis was given to academic standards and to the training of experts. The educational system again became a competitive one in which only the privileged could succeed. With the renewed emphasis on academic performance, the children of the proletariat who had to spend time looking after their siblings and helping in production were at a disadvantage; the chances for workers and peasants to obtain an education were further lessened.

The aim in closing down the irregular schools had been to raise academic standards and reports indicated that this was achieved. The marks of students in one middle school, for example, were 33 percent higher than those of 1959.[39] Because of the grossness of such estimates and the subjectivity attached to grading, the real extent of improved education is difficult to assess. Judging from the greater attention given to academic learning, one has to admit that, compared with the GLF, a great amount of learning activity is likely to have taken place. Whether it eventually contributed to socialist reconstruction remains an open question.

At the university level, more research was carried out. Tsinghua University alone reported that 190 research projects were completed and 210 papers written in one year.[40] These papers included studies in the history of the development of chemistry, in the history of inventions in mechanical engineering, and in the theory of the elasticity of double layer structures. These figures, however, reflect a mechanical approach to implementation. Progress in research was still reckoned according to quantity and not quality. Given the abstruse nature of many of these studies, their value to socialist reconstruction is debatable.

If the expertise acquired by the younger generation was to contribute to socialist reconstruction they would have to be willing to provide their services in places where their skills were most required and it appeared that they were reluctant to do so. Although socialist ideological education within the schools was still officially approved, in effect it had been replaced by subtle ideological education of a bourgeois nature, emphasizing individualism, competition, expertise, and the separation of mental from manual labour, of theory from practice. Rewards went to the academically advanced rather than to the ideologically progressive. Students with good grades received special honours. Those professors with a high academic output enjoyed greater prestige and were deferred to by the administrators in professional matters, giving them a position of leadership. The examples provided by these professors and the rewards accruing to the academically 'advanced' students would seem destined to influence the outlook of the younger generation, encouraging them to strive for academic achievement rather than ideological 'redness', to consider personal gain above their contribution to socialist construction.

The structural characteristics which nurtured this spirit of individualism and academic output were by no means new. They were the remnants of the pre-liberation educational system that had been left intact since 1949 and which during the GLF had effectively thwarted the intentions of the leaders to create an educational system more in tune with the socialist society. Moreover, in the absence of policies to check their growth, these tendencies continued to thrive in the sixties.

As the status of the intellectuals grew, they began to complain of the lack of respect shown them. The following letter published in a newspaper probably echoed the sentiments of many intellectuals. 'Concerning the implementation of the policy in respect to the intellectuals, some comrades hold one-sided views about intellectuals, have failed to show them due respect for the labour of teachers and their expertise, have expected too much from and had been too impatient with teachers in their transformation, have failed to cooperate with teachers closely enough.'[41] There may be some truth in this statement. But there was probably even more truth in this description during the GLF than in 1962. This complaint came when the prestige of the intellectuals was on the rise, showing they were now secure enough to voice their dissatisfaction. More important, the deference to experts strengthened the control the traditional elites had on education. Their obtaining a platform to disseminate their views on individualism and expertise enabled them to influence the younger generation, and only those who internalized and abided by their philosophy were rewarded with the chance of higher education and an elitist position later on in life. The educational system provided the elites with a training ground for their successors and perpetuated their existence as a collectivity.

Economic developments during this period also encouraged the growth of capitalist tendencies in education, providing a fertile ground for the growth and support of bourgeois values. The increasing attention given to raising produce for market on private plots and growing speculation in such markets further nurtured individualism and competition in the larger society. Not only were managerial and technical personnel attaining higher status and greater financial returns, they were now to be recruited exclusively from the full-time schools.[42] This encouraged academic pursuits and further strengthened the superior position of the regular schools, compared to the irregular ones. It benefited particularly those from the landlord or business background who had greater access to the regular schools and who could now assume organizational legitimacy based on their expertise.

The unfolding of events in this period again demonstrates the crucial role played by implementers and by objective conditions in shaping development. At this time, vigilance against the proliferation of capitalist tendencies lessened. In spite of the intention of the policies to promote socialism, the tendencies towards capitalism were strengthened in a way unanticipated by the hegemonic group, demonstrating the resilience of capitalist structures in a socialist regime, as well as capitalism's role in retarding socialist development. It became increasingly apparent that this educational system was a breeding ground for a new type of elite who based their power not so much on their class background as on their monopolization of expertise. The traditional elites still existed, only now, in the socialist era, taking a different form. The weaknesses that the educational policies of the GLF set out to eliminate had returned in full measure with the widening gap between theory and practice, mental and manual labour, and the rural and urban areas. Ultimately, the recognition of what had occurred led to a struggle within the hegemonic group, to a deliberate attempt to 'smash' the capitalist structures, which culminated in the Cultural Revolution.

Prelude to the
Cultural Revolution:
January 1963–August 1966

Economic conditions gradually improved in the early sixties. In 1962, China fulfilled her industrial quota ahead of schedule, and in January 1963, appeared the first optimistic statement on agriculture in three years: 'The year 1962 has ended. The rural areas in China passed this year in struggle and in triumph. Although the rural areas in China have been stricken in the past year, the like of which has never happened in the past century, a very good harvest, better than that of 1961, was reaped in 1962.'[1] Conditions continued to get better over the next four years. The grain output of 1963 topped that of 1962, and the cotton crop was up by 20 percent. The economic output of 1964 was equally encouraging. The deputy minister of agriculture reported that '1964 was a good year for Chinese agriculture. After increases in both 1962 and 1963, still better harvests, equal to those of the high yield years of the past, were won'.[2] Industrial output was assessed as being 15 percent above the previous year. And in 1965, the agricultural output of grain, cotton, and oil-bearing crops continued on an upward trend. In industry, the rate of development surpassed by a clear margin the target set in the 1965 state budget.[3] The country was prepared to launch the Third Five Year Plan.

Of equal importance to production in the socialist economy are the social relations of production. During the GLF, the tendencies towards capitalism had been deliberately curbed by mass mobilization and state intervention in trade and property ownership. In the early sixties, with the emphasis on coordination, material incentives, and reliance on experts, capitalist tendencies again came to the fore. Although no statistics on increases in private enterprise are available, reports indicate that it was definitely on the rise. In 1965, the following passage appeared in the *People's*

Daily: 'Beginning in 1963, subsidiary occupations in rural areas have been speedily restored and developed. But development is by no means balanced. While private subsidiary occupations have developed quickly, those for the collectives have developed slowly.'4 This growth of private subsidiary industries in the rural areas had a tremendous impact on existing class divisions in China. Since the wealthier peasants still possessed better tools, better land, and more capital, they were in a better position to capitalize on the resurgence of private industrial and agricultural pursuits.

Raising goods and selling them privately in turn led to neglect of the collective plots. Even the manure needed to fertilize collective plots tended to be diverted to private holdings. The result was a lowering in the collective income, further widening the gap between rich and poor. Those peasants who depended solely on collective income were, of course, the worst off.

With the increasing emphasis put on profit, workers in industries sometimes refused to take up jobs that were comparatively poorly paid. Self-interest showed up everywhere. In some instances, members of the organizing committees gave themselves more work points than were warranted. In one case, the team leader, recorder, and accountant allotted themselves 6 percent of the collective income! On occasion, leaders of productive teams worked on public plots for their own private profit.

The profit motive even dominated the running of public enterprises, some refusing to set quotas for producing goods which yielded little profit. Others voluntarily folded as soon as the market price for their products dropped and reduced the profit margin: 'Since last summer, [with] a drop in the price of live pigs, ... some people considered pig raising not so profitable as before and immediately sold their stocks. Some teams also showed a lack of interest in collective pig raising, as they regarded it as less rewarding than the other more profitable enterprises.'5 Maintaining the general supply of goods had been superseded by the profit motive.

Accompanying the upsurge in private enterprise was an increasing bureaucratization in the organization of labour. Because of the overall emphasis on coordination, planning, accounting, and administration, cadres tended to devote their time solely to administrative matters and had minimum contact with the masses.

Often, while the number of meetings proliferated, the original intention to study objective conditions before making overall plans was neglected. In their planning of enterprises, cadres pursued expansion and comprehensiveness, imitating foreign countries rather than taking into consideration local requirements. As a result, instead of remedying the deficiencies of the GLF, its lack of planning and the formulation of unrealistic targets, administrators moved to the other extreme, planning large enterprises that in the end were not necessarily suited to local needs.

While material incentives and dependence on experts were intended to raise production, this Liuist strategy also encouraged the renewed growth of an elite. It was in this sense in particular that Liuist policy was bourgeois. It was more than ten years after liberation. Recruitment into positions of responsibility was now based not so much on one's revolutionary zeal as on one's expertise as measured by educational qualifications. Because those from the landlord or business background had the financial backing and the supportive home environment to put them through the competitive educational system based on academic achievement, they in particular benefited; through their possession of expertise their positions of power were secured.

The division of responsibility is perhaps inevitable in any society requiring a complex organization of labour, but it is not in itself conducive to the growth of an elite. Only when positions of responsibility are accompanied by an unchecked and growing trend to higher status and better income does it become detrimental to the socialist society. The development of these trends in China in the sixties provided the basis for the appearance of a new elite whose power was not based on the possession of private property but on the monopoly of expertise, and divided society into a new type of haves and have-nots. The traditional elites had taken a new form. It was the emergence of this special category in all sectors of society, including the party, that moved Mao to make his counter-attacks.

If one assumes there is a purely mechanical relationship between the economy and education, then one would also expect that, with the improvement in conditions in the early sixties, existing economic and educational policies would have been continued. But this was not the case. When the economy improved, and academic standards within the schools had been raised, another set of policies was formulated in the mid-sixties which conflicted with the existing ones, showing that educational policies are not necessarily formulated as a direct response to the level of production. The changes in the educational as well as economic policies during this period appear to have resulted from reactions to the increasingly apparent capitalist characteristics in the social relations in the economy as well as in education.

REACTIONS OF THE POLICY-MAKERS

Developments in the mid-sixties also demonstrate the important role of political alliance in educational development. Between 1958 and 1962, there had been a near consensus both within the hegemonic group and among the implementers. During the next three years, factions supporting differing strategies of development emerged and vied for dominance, the main choice being between capitalizing on existing programs to raise the level of production and accepting a slowing rate of economic growth, but curbing capitalist tendencies. Even though economic conditions were relatively stable, it was shifts in what was now a delicate balance of power that led to changes in both the economic and educational policies.

Growing recognition of the capitalist tendencies proliferating as a result of the Liuist policies of consolidation and retrenchment led to a gradual shift of alliance in favour of the Maoist strategy of development. Liu also recognized that the social forces unleashed during the Period of Retrenchment made the situation critical, but he disagreed with Mao as to how they should be curbed. Mao favoured changes from below; Liu, an imposition of greater party control. Liu valued highly the contribution of the experts and felt that differential pay according to skill was not a deviation from communist ideology.[6] Bourgeois rights or the entitlement to privileges by virtue of one's skill or expertise emerged as a major controversial issue. It was Liu's refusal to abandon his policy of exclusive reliance on experts and his unreserved acceptance of bourgeois rights that led to the final rift between him and Mao, culminating in Liu's being branded as a bourgeois renegade during the Cultural Revolution (1966–68).

Details of the shifting alliances during this period are not available, but much can be pieced together from various events that occurred from 1962 on. While Liu Shao-ch'i and P'eng Chen pushed for the rehabilitation of P'eng Te-huai in 1962, their efforts did not achieve any concrete result, indicating that the power of the Maoist opposition was still considerable.[7] Then, at the tenth plenary session of the Eighth Party Congress in September 1962, the policy of 'three selfs and one guarantee' came under attack and the 'Socialist Education Movement' to weed out 'bourgeois' power-holders was formally launched. The people were reminded that class struggle still existed in a socialist society:

Members of the reactionary class which has been overthrown are not reconciled to their doom. They always attempt to stage a comeback. Meanwhile, there still exists in society a bourgeois influence, the force of habit of the old society and the tendency towards capitalism among the small producers. Therefore, among the people, a small number of persons, making up only a tiny fraction of the total population, who have not yet undergone socialist remoulding, always attempt to depart from the socialist road and turn to the capitalist road whenever there is an opportunity. Class struggle is inevitable under these circumstances.[8]

This communiqué was probably drafted by the Maoist faction, but the fact that no direct or personal allegations were made indicates perhaps that neither side was able to overpower the other, and no direct confrontation seems to have occurred between the two leaders, Liu and Mao.

Liu, as chairman of the Republic, had occupied the limelight since 1959, receiving foreign guests and prime ministers and conducting the affairs of state. But in 1962, Mao staged a comeback. Perhaps as part of the political ploy to capture public opinion and direct attention to the causes he fought for, Mao put in many public appearances at performances staged by revolutionary theatre and opera companies, publicizing his support of art and literature that portrayed the proletariat rather than the elite.

Both sought to appeal to a large audience through their publications. On August 1, 1962, Liu reprinted *How to be a Good Communist*, his book on self-discipline and the role of the party organization. The audience for this work were mainly party members who used it in their political study in 1963, perhaps showing that Liu's power base lay within the party bureaucracy. In the same year, in the introduction to 'The Draft Decision of the CCPCC on Central Problems of our Rural Work' Mao wrote:

> Generally speaking, those [policies, ideas] that succeed are correct and those that fail are incorrect, and this is especially true of man's struggle with nature. In social struggle, the forces representing the advanced class sometimes suffer defeat not because their ideas are incorrect but because in the balance of forces engaged in struggle they are not powerful for the time being as the force of reaction; they are therefore temporarily defeated but they are found to triumph through the test of time.[9]

This statement perhaps encapsulated Mao's apologetics for the temporary failure of the GLF and offered a reminder of the necessity to review the correctness of a policy in terms not only of its immediate successes, but of its direction. It also served as a warning to assess the Liuist line not only in raising the level of production but in its contribution to socialist construction. In the same period, the works of Mao were widely disseminated. Lin Piao promoted the study of Mao's works within the PLA, and later, among the masses.

The struggle was not confined to rivalry between the two leaders, however. It involved other top decision-makers as well. Support for the Liuist policy, especially in the cultural and academic circles, remained strong. Among Liu's most influential supporters were Chou Yang, the party propagandist, Teng To, editor of the *Frontline*, and Yang Hsien-chen, instructor of the party school. Others included presidents and first secretaries of the universities of Wuhan, Chungshan, Nanking, and Chengchow.

Again, it would be difficult to establish whether there was any conspiracy between Liu and these intellectuals. According to Dittmer, the events of the Cultural Revolution pointed to connections between intellectuals based in Peking and P'eng Chen, but not to Liu. Liu's failing was that, in remaining aloof while in charge of the state, he unwittingly connived with those intellectuals representing capitalist and 'corrupt' tendencies.[10] In any event, the works of these intellectuals did provide the philosophical underpinnings for the policies of Liu. Yang Hsien-chen, in his theory of 'two combined into one', emphasized the unity of opposites, minimizing the role of class struggle in the process of change, and advocating compromise. This theory had strong political implications, for Yang's ideas were disseminated among party members, raising the possibility of a return to capitalism. Sun Yeh-fang, the director of the Chinese Academy of Sciences' Research Institute of Economics, advocated a policy of 'balanced development' and 'the primacy of efficiency'. The policy of balanced development, in practice, encouraged the proliferation of private enterprise. The primacy of efficiency provided theoretical support to the idea that the pursuit of profit in private and public enterprise rather than in the provision of goods for mass consumption was essential to Chinese economic development.[11]

Because Liu's power base was among the intellectuals, it was on the ideological front that the Maoists directed their attack. Indeed, the Cultural Revolution started as a series of newspaper debates on Teng To's view that the morality of the feudal era was applicable to the socialist society. Discussions and debates also centred around Wu Han's play *Dismissal of Hai Jui* and Yang Hsien-cheng's theory of 'two combined into one'. Both Teng To and Yang Hsien-cheng were party spokesmen on the philosophical front. Teng To had been the editor of the *People's Daily* since 1954 and then transferred to *Frontline* in 1959, and Yang was the director of the Philosophy Department of the party school since the Yenan Days, perhaps reflecting the extent to which the bourgeois ideology had infiltrated to top party ranks.

Since Liuist supporters were strong in the cultural arena and controlled the mass media, many of the articles criticizing their theories were at first suppressed. The article written by Yao Wen-Yuan criticizing *Dismissal of Hai Jui*, for example, was published in *Wen-hui Pao*, a Shanghai newspaper, in November 1965, but it was not printed in Peking until it had been reproduced in several provincial newspapers and the *PLA Daily*.

In line with Maoist principles, the masses were mobilized in the struggle, tilting the balance of power in Mao's favour. However, Liu's position remained strong for a considerable time, Mao being unable to gain a decisive victory. The only indication that a number of others in the upper reaches of the echelon might also be involved in the struggle comes from an editorial that appeared in the reorganized *Peking Daily* after Liu's supporters in the newspaper were purged:

> There are also some units where the leaders resist the movement by the methods of sham mobilization but real suppression, sham leadership but real resistance. If these people do not hold their reins on the brink of the precipice and wake up, they will certainly be dragged out by the revolutionary masses, their names will be made public in the newspaper, they will be dismissed from their official posts, and their authority will be seized from them. They will be knocked down and disgraced.[12]

ECONOMIC POLICY

Parallelling the shifting power balance within the hegemonic group was a gradual shift in China's economic policies, from an emphasis on management, planning, and mechanization back to the Maoist principles of mass line, mass mobilization, and ideological motivation. But the victory of neither faction was complete; the uneasy balance of power was reflected in the many internal contradictions in the new policies. On the one hand, economic policies emphasized self-reliance, conservation, mass initiative, and ideological motivation; on the other, they defended and encouraged the use of key-points and material incentives.

Throughout this period, there was no change in the overall policy guidelines. Agriculture was still seen as the foundation of the national economy, and industry as its support. Po I-po wrote an article which appeared in the *Peking Review*:

> Agriculture forms the foundation for the growth of our industry and the whole national economy. The basic means of subsistence of our population of over 600 million is met mainly by agriculture as the foundation of the development of the national economy.

On the role of industry, he wrote:

All industry, whether light or heavy must make the country-side its principal market. Heavy industry in particular must regard supporting the technical reform of agriculture as its foremost task, and must see to it that socialist industrialization and the modernization of agriculture are closely integrated and help each other forward.[13]

However there was a shift in the strategies of development. In early 1963, a statement in the *Kuang-ming Daily* reported that: 'the task on our industrial front will be, as required by the tenth plenary session of the Eighth Central Committee of the Party, to continue implementing the policies of readjustment, consolidation, supplementation, planning, and arrangement of the direction of production, and the policy to bring industrial work properly in line, with agriculture as the foundation.'[14] With the close of the fourth session of the second National People's Congress, there was a different note on the development of China. On December 4, the *People's Daily* reported on the close of the session:

> The session pointed out with satisfaction that under the leadership of the CCP and Chairman Mao Tse-tung, and guided by the general line of comprehensive development aiming high, and achieving faster, better, and more economic results in building socialism—the people of all nationalities in the country have greatly raised and developed their socialist consciousness, political enthusiasm, and labour initiative; and during the Second Five Year Plan period and in 1963, won brilliant victories in the socialist revolution and socialist construction. In those periods, a big leap has been made by our country toward building an independent, complete, and modern national economy.[15]

The tone of the second of these reports had completely changed. The first still emphasized organization, planning, management. The second embodied a view of development similar to that of the GLF, increasing socialist consciousness, political enthusiasm, and labour initiative in the service of the nation. The guideline of 'readjustment, consolidation, supplementation, and perfection' was replaced by 'comprehensive development, aiming high, and achieving faster, better, and more economic results', indicating the growing ascendency of the Maoists.

The mentality that slavishly followed foreign concepts and ignored local conditions was extensively criticized. For example, some officials who constructed a V-shaped steel mill that was claimed to accommodate twenty-four hour shifts were criticized for failing to consider sufficiently the existing local requirements of such a building in their blind pursuit of bigness. The V-shaped building took up too much space and the weather conditions would not permit night shifts. The emphasis now was on 'self-reliance'—Chinese solutions to Chinese problems.

In the *Peking Review*, Po I-po asserted this view:

Every socialist country should rely mainly on itself for its construction.... In our socialist industrialization, it is only by relying on the diligent labour of our people, making full use of our country's rich resources and bringing all our potential into play that we can rapidly establish our powerful industry, build an independent, comprehensive, and modern industrial system, create a powerful material and technical foundation for the entire economy, further consolidate our country and constantly raise the people's living standards.[16]

The necessity for self-reliance had become more important with the withdrawal of Russian aid in 1962, but in this period, self-reliance meant reliance on the masses and local resources rather than on technology and expertise. 'The "spirit of the cent" became a catch phrase; it meant: the spirit of conserving every single cent and making minute calculations, as well as the earnest work style of making deep penetration without compromise on small details. ... Without this spirit and work style, an enormous increase in the economy is impossible.'[17] Cadres in particular were reminded to cut expenditures and make the best use of existing resources. Again, this spirit was reminiscent of the GLF and its anti-waste campaign.

To make 'deep penetration without compromise on small details', the cadres were exhorted to consult the common people before making decisions: 'To follow the mass line, it is necessary to trust and rely on the masses consciously and seriously, to discuss everything with them and to collect their opinions as well.

This makes it necessary to correct the method of merely listening to the opinions of the cadres and discussing things with them. To consult only the cadres and neglect the masses is a cadre line, not the mass line."[18] By focusing on the needs of the people, the weaknesses of formulating plans irrelevant to existing conditions could be corrected. By replacing vertical management with mass mobilization, marginal resources could be utilized. Collective action could transform socialist ideals into reality.

The preoccupation with profit also came under attack. A system based on profit and material incentives would lead to graft, speculation, stockpiling, higher prices, and corruption.[19] Business enterprises within the socialist society once again were to produce essential goods. It was emphasized that the difference between socialist and capitalist enterprises lay in their political outlook.

In order to operate a socialist enterprise successfully, it is absolutely necessary to put politics in command, with class struggle and the struggle between the two roads as the mainstay. An enterprise which departs from politics and exclusively pursues profit will inevitably change from a socialist into a capitalist enterprise. ... The standard by which to measure the good or poor work of an enterprise is whether it brings politics to the fore, whether it is operated strictly in accordance with the thought of Mao Tse-tung ..., the primary task of our industrial factories is to foster and train proletarian, revolutionary workers with the thoughts of Mao Tse-tung.[20]

To nurture the proletarian outlook and increase production, mass movements to raise the socialist consciousness were again launched. As during the GLF, these movements penetrated every sector of society—including the party, the bureaucracy, and the schools. All were asked to learn from the PLA: their discipline, ideology, and emphasis on social action. Lei Feng, a PLA member idealized as living up to the thoughts of Mao Tse-tung and dying while on duty, was a figure to be emulated by all. Books by Mao were widely disseminated and the people were asked to learn from them. In industries and agriculture, advanced units which solved their problems through mass mobilization were widely publicized. Taching, a thriving oil-producing community, became an example to be emulated by other industrial units. Tachai, which cleared and irrigated farmlands in spite of repeated damage from natural disasters, provided a model for agricultural units. The slogan was 'to compare with, learn from, catch up, and overtake the advanced, and to help the less advanced'. Work units all over the country organized their cadres to visit the advanced units and learn from them. Representatives from the advanced units visited the more backward ones to exchange ideas and help them. It is true that a spirit of competition still prevailed. But unlike the previous period, the goal of competition now was to strive for the collective good, rather than for individual profit and achievement. Cooperation was to replace individualism.

However, the Maoist line did not completely oust the Liuist policy. Conflicting tendencies could still be found. There was the administrative policy of 'squatting at a point' which meant, essentially, the development and consolidation of the advanced units before the dissemination of the policy elsewhere. This policy ran counter to the current emphasis on mass mobilization. According to accusations made during the Cultural Revolution, Liu Shao-ch'i and his wife effectively quashed a 'Socialist Education Movement' while they 'squatted' at Taoyuan, and in their investigation, shifted the responsibility for the proliferation of capitalist tendencies to the lower cadres.

The use of material incentives was not completely absent either. In an effort to raise technological development, the State Council, in October 1963, passed the Regulations on the Awards for Invention and Technical Improvement. 'These two sets of regulations indicate once again the great attention paid by the party and government to inventions and technical improvements and to the encouragement and support of the broad masses.'[21] Cash bonuses were offered for worthwhile inventions. Awards ranged from $10,000 for inventions down to $1,000 for technical improvements. Once again, material incentives were being used. In an editorial accompanying the passing of these regulations, the role of the experts was again emphasized:

Some young workers or apprentices may perhaps hold that since their technical level is low they can do nothing to bring about technical improvement. We hold that, provided they take heed of what the Party says and are willing to learn humbly from the veteran workers, and to study hard, young people are also able to bring about successes in technical improvements. Even though they make no new creations or technical inventions, provided that they study actively and are skilful in making use of the inventions and technical improvements already achieved, they are also doing something concrete to show they are making improvement in production and are engaged in creative labour.[22]

The Maoist would perhaps disagree with the prediction that the uneducated workers could never produce new inventions.

As late as December 1965, an editorial in the *People's Daily*, the party propaganda organ, defended the presence of family business sidelines in the socialist economy.[23] It stated that commune members who worked on private plots did not own the principal means of production—land—and therefore were not capitalists, again raising the issue of bourgeois rights and to what extent they should now be curbed. The defence of the existence of these private plots for individual use 'on a long-term basis' clearly indicated that resistance to the rooting out of private enterprise was still entrenched.

EDUCATIONAL POLICY

Like economic policies, educational policies were marked by contradictions. They were tailored to overcome the weaknesses that had become increasingly apparent during the Period of Retrenchment, as well as to meet the new demands of the changing economy. Given the contradictions in the latter, it is only logical that they would also be reflected in the educational policies.

Education was perceived as an important institution in the maintenance of the economic base through its role in installing socialist consciousness and culture. The following statement of Mao's was constantly cited as a justification for educational policies, whether they conformed to his basic theories or not: 'Our educational policy should enable those who receive education to make progress morally, culturally, intellectually, and physically, in order to become workers with a socialist consciousness.[24] There was general consensus within the leading group that education was to train revolutionary successors who were both 'red and expert', but owing to the different emphases put on these two traits, the issue of training revolutionary successors became a source of contention.

The policy-makers remained preoccupied with the quality of education well into the sixties. In 1962, the *People's Daily* carried an editorial urging the improvement in the quality of primary and secondary schools: 'The quality of middle and primary schools will also have an effect on the level of specialized education and scientific research. The development of the cause of socialism in our country requires us to train more and better experts and scientific and technical personnel in the various fields from the new generation.'[25] On the other hand it warned: 'It would be one-sided and wrong to overlook intellectual education and academic achievements of the students'.[26] With this end in view, the Ministry of Education organized a forum for the middle school teachers in Peking to discuss teaching and examination methods shortly afterward. Similar meetings were held in the provinces. As late as 1965, an article which discussed the importance of the task of bringing up successors of the proletarian revolution thus elaborated: 'In the course of educating teenagers and children ... it is necessary to take the guidance of teenagers and children to learn culture and scientific knowledge vigorously and actively as a very important task and perform it very seriously. ... Politics is not an abstract thing and it must be demonstrated concretely through professional work.'[27] Even late in 1965, the priority in the training of revolutionary successors was given to the development of professional skill, again reflecting the fact that the educational system was one of the last bastions of power of the traditional elites, who were greatly influenced by the emphasis on the training of experts in the pre-liberation period.

In late 1965, Mao came out in direct attack of the existing system. In a famous talk in Hanchow, he criticized the irrelevance of the curriculum, the exclusive attention paid to theoretical studies, the unfair system of admission, the seclusion of the students, and the burden of the examination system.[28] In short, the educational system was 'murdering' the students. Perhaps as a response to these criticisms, some policy statements appeared which indicated that the emphasis on academic quality was to be replaced by an all-round conception of education. The work load of the students was too heavy. The new line was 'less but finer'. That is, students should have lighter work loads to enable them to take more time to develop culturally and physically: 'Teaching reforms are being developed in depth. Many schools have intensified their ideological and political work and effected a closer integration of education and productive labour. Some schools have already begun to enforce the principles of 'less but finer', with the aim of enabling the students to gain greater initiative for their all-round development, morally, intellectually, and physically.[29] While it is true that the emphasis on academic studies gave way to an all-round concept of education, the meaning attached to 'less and finer', like that attached to 'unity of theory and practice', could in practice very easily be taken to mean specialization, in-depth analysis of specialized areas.

On the other hand, there was pressure to universalize education. This meant an increase in the number of schools and also a more rational distribution of opportunities, to bridge the gap between the urban and rural areas. 'In the course of implementing the Party's educational guidelines and the universalizing of rural elementary education, it is necessary not only to increase continuously the number of schools and students according to requirements and possibilities, but also to pay prompt attention to solving problems concerning the distribution of schools.'[30]

The value of the irregular schools was re-affirmed. A report on the national conference held in January 1964 stated: 'The conference decided that this form of education should be extended vigorously for the next two years. It is intended to raise the political, cultural, and technical levels of the workers rapidly to meet the increasing needs of national construction.'[31] In 1965, Ho Wei, the minister of education, defended the agricultural schools and outlined what should be done to promote them:

Rural students now constitute more than 80 percent of the total number of students in our country. To conduct rural education well is of decisive significance to changing the appearance of our country's educational undertaking as a whole. How can we conduct rural education well? The most fundamental thing to do is to hold high the red banner of the thoughts of Mao Tse-tung and implement the directive of the Party centre and Comrade Liu Shao-ch'i concerning two labour systems and two education systems. This means we should energetically and experimentally operate part farming, part study schools well—in this way promoting the revolutionization and development of rural education in a more healthy and more penetrating manner.[32]

Statements such as these are significant, for they indicate a renewed interest in the work/study schools, which had been shelved since 1960. Ho Wei's statement also shows a shift of attention from the urban back to the rural areas, marking a triumph for the Maoist line. Even Lu Ting-i, who had once advocated shelving the irregular schools, came out in their support. The Maoist victory, however, was not yet complete. Mao saw these schools as an embodiment of socialist ideology; Liu, however, as late as 1965, emphasized the economic contributions they could make: 'The money needed to run a full-time school can run four to five work/study schools, and the demand of the students for higher schooling can be met to a fuller extent'.[33] Oddly enough, the new guidelines for educational development were attributed to both Liu and Mao, although each in fact advocated a different line. Again this indicates the uneasy balance of power at the centre. The two leaders had come into conflict not only over the economy, but also over education.

Another attempt to redistribute educational opportunities was the policy of 'from the commune and back to the commune'. The members of the production brigade within the communes were to make a careful selection from their members and recommend them to the agricultural schools or universities. These students would receive 70 percent of their monthly pay, and on finishing their studies, would then return to their place of origin to work. The intent of this policy was to ensure a more equal distribution of educational opportunities, giving the children of the poor and middle-class peasants more chance to gain a higher education. It also ensured that the ideologically advanced would be provided opportunities of education, in spite of their low cultural level, and that the dissatisfaction of those graduates who did not wish to be sent to the countryside was eliminated. This policy could be regarded as a first attempt to reform the admission procedures in the educational system. The policy of recommendation into institutes of higher learning after the Cultural Revolution was perhaps patterned after this.

Like her economic policies, Chinese educational policies reaffirmed the need for self-reliance and 'walking on two legs.' One editorial pointed out that the failure of the people-run schools was because 'some authorities pay serious attention only to the operation of full time schools, but not to simple schools in different forms. They pay serious attention only to the government operated schools, but not to schools operated by the people on a private basis.' The same editorial urged: 'We must consult them [the masses] when their opinions are needed and give full play to their enthusiasm for the operation of schools. Only by doing so, can we do our work well and solve smoothly some concrete problems in the operation of schools.'[34] The schools were referred to as 'people-run schools' perhaps to focus attention on the active role of the masses. Through community effort and official support, it was hoped that schools would be established in areas where there was great demand and development had been neglected.

The educational policies during the sixties were not embodied in any comprehensive directive such as those publicized in September 1958. It might be interpreted as a sign of continuing bureaucratization during this period, for direction continued to flow from the policy-makers to the implementers, and the masses still were excluded from the running of their schools. Directives were usually transmitted through the educational bureaucracy to the individual cadres involved. It could also be an indication that, among the decision-makers, there was insufficient support or consensus to promulgate a single, comprehensive guideline. The Maoist educational policies were not yet in complete ascendance.

IMPLEMENTATION

Nonetheless, there were interesting developments at the implementation level. In the fifties and early sixties, the cadres, administrators, and educated intellectuals were the most vocal in expressing their objections. Although the intent during the GLF was to increase educational facilities and programs through mass effort, in fact, the setting up of new schools seemed to be confined to the cadres and intellectuals. There is little or no evidence of initiative coming from the peasants, who remained suspicious of any but the traditional type of school. In the early sixties, the role of the parents in socializing their young was recognized, and while their activities then were relatively passive, being mainly confined to attendance at parents' meetings organized by the schools and listening to explanations of party policies or exhortations to encourage their children to go to the countryside, a more spontaneous and positive response from the population began to emerge at this time.

The cumulative effect of the recent educational reforms began to be felt in the mid-sixties. The people began to express resentment at their exclusion from running the schools. Peasants started writing to the newspapers—a departure that might reflect the growing literacy of the rural population. In general, their letters expressed support for the work/study schools which, by 1963, were sending out their graduates to the communes where they were generally well received. Opinions were expressed that they were better adjusted and more useful than students from the regular schools since they already possessed the basic agricultural skills and could contribute much to the communes as technicians, tractor drivers, farmers, work point recorders, accountants, and even team leaders.[35]

The peasants' letters also expressed displeasure with some of the officials. They exposed corrupt practices among the cadres with regard to work points, criticized them for excluding peasant children from the regular schools, and accused them of unreasonably adhering to rules. One peasant from Hunan, for example, wrote that his daughter was sometimes late for school because she had to help with the housework. He complained that: 'The so-called headmaster and the teacher of this school took advantage of this and forced her to give up her studies with the false accusation that she was undisciplined and poor in study.'[36] On another occasion, the same peasant was unable to pay tuition because of the serious drought of the previous year. He paid in part, but for half a term the school would not issue textbooks to his daughter. Finally, he went to talk to the teachers personally, but without result. Only when the party cadre went in person did the school relent.

The students were also becoming more vocal, expressing a variety of opinions. In 1965, one wrote to the *Kuang-ming Daily* that: 'As early as my junior school days, some teachers and schoolmates and other persons tried unceasingly to instil into me bourgeois ideas of personal fame and material benefit. Many books also disseminated the bourgeois ideology of personal fame and material benefit.'[37] Others criticized the irrelevance of the curriculum. One law student from Peking University complained that he had to learn the Soviet Penal Code, to which he never again referred, once he went out to work. Some criticized the number of mandatory extra-curricular activities during the summer, which deprived them even of the time to rest or to fulfil their summer assignments. Other students voiced opinions that were in conflict with the socialist ideology. Some expressed their dislike for agricultural work, claiming that it was not honourable for students who had spent ten years in school to work on the land; they would soon forget what they had learned.[38]

Though some were influenced by the ideology of the bourgeois class, many became the vanguards for the Cultural Revolution in 1966. These were the ones who criticized teachers and university presidents, the traditional embodiment of authority. At the beginning of the Cultural Revolution, the situation was in a state of confusion. The resistance to such criticism at the centre was strong. Many students who criticized the authorities or the party were themselves purged or dismissed. It required a high degree of commitment to the socialist ideology to take up the revolutionary cause at this stage.

At the administrative level, there were also divisions among the cadres. In the early sixties, newspaper articles, written by protagonists of the Liuist line, supporting existing policies, were usually interspersed with dissenting voices from the Maoist camp. Gradually the defenders of Liu were silenced, indicating the growing power of Mao.

These newspaper discussions were mostly confined to philosophy, art, and literature. In education, the debate centred on the load of school work that should be shouldered by the students, the number of extra-curricular activities in which they should participate, and the amount of rest they should have. At this time, neither the existing structure of the educational system nor the relevance of the curriculum was ever questioned. It was only when the students were mobilized that the discussions became more heated and basic educational issues were raised. The continuing general acceptance of the status quo in education among the implementers helped to explain why Liu's policy, which concentrated on improving the regular schools, received the greatest support for so long; in face of such opposition, Mao's efforts to introduce an alternative model encountered considerable resistance for some years.

During the Cultural Revolution it was revealed that some of the implementers had sabotaged attempts to pursue the policy to integrate theory with practice and to establish work/study schools. Cadres from some of the educational departments at the local level were accused of having forcibly closed down such schools, on the alleged grounds that they were neither schools nor work teams. Claims were also made that experiments on the integration of theory with practice had been criticized by many administrators. Lu Ping, the president of Peking University, for example, was accused of having discouraged the mathematics department from pursuing this policy, as well as having prevented the incorporation of the thoughts of Mao into the political course.[39]

Because of the implementers' widespread faith in the traditional educational system and in the pursuit of technical skills and cultural knowledge, even well-intentioned reforms to make the existing system more socialist in tone could not be realized. The educational reforms introduced appeared piecemeal, did not have any radical impact, and were often bogged down by internal contradictions in the system. It became increasingly clear to the Maoist faction that the power of the existing implementers had to be shattered, and that the students had to be involved if any basic change was to be effected.

Changing Administrative Style
To curb the trend towards increasing bureaucratization, school administrators now made serious attempts to simplify their meetings and to integrate with the masses. In the schools, cadres made deliberate efforts to talk with the teachers and exchange experiences with them. The number of meetings was cut down to allow time to meet with the teachers. In a primary school in Shang-

hai, several administrators 'set up contacts with one or two teaching research teams ... regularly prepared for class and attended class together with teachers and chatted with them individually'. To cut down the number of meetings, the same school stipulated that: 'Meetings of teachers are generally held from three to five in the afternoon. Some meetings of cadres may last longer, but they must not drag beyond six o'clock at the latest.'[40]

On the other hand, the strategies used in industries: 'squatting at a point' and 'using key units' were adopted in education. According to these strategies: 'A small number of middle and primary schools with comparatively strong leadership, good teachers, and good equipment should be chosen as key schools to be well run, thus forming the backbone of full-day middle and primary schools and acting as examples to other schools in general. Simultaneously, efforts must be exerted to make a success of all existing public-run, full-day middle and primary schools in the province.'[41] Conferences were held for the dissemination of new ideas. Advanced units became examples to be emulated. At first, cadres organized agricultural or spare-time schools in key areas where there were favourable conditions, gradually increasing the number when these schools were consolidated. The first conference of the work/study schools was held in 1965 to permit the different units to exchange ideas. Yutsai Middle School in Shanghai became the advanced unit in education to be emulated by other schools. The strategy was 'to compare, learn from, overtake, and catch up with the advanced'.

The reliance on key units led to a more cautious approach in the implementation of educational guidelines. This policy had its inherent contradiction. It curtailed the involvement of the masses, putting the onus on the leadership. Further, the key schools had better facilities than the others and sometimes developed into special schools for relatives of the party and administrative cadres. As a consequence, the key schools came under attack during the Cultural Revolution.

Raising the Quality of Education
In the primary and secondary schools all over the country, teachers and administrators busily engaged in reforming educational practice within the system. In Shanghai, it was reported that:

The idea of a single-minded pursuit of a high percentage of promotion has been waived; the situation of cramming in classrooms has changed and the mechanical method of teaching has been somewhat repudiated; the situation whereby students are oppressed by tests and examinations has changed and some schools have started to improve their methods of examination. With the load of assignments lightened, the ideological and political education of students has been intensified. Particularly since the teaching of political science was transformed, close attention has been paid to implementing the principle of integrating theory with practice, and importance has been attached to grasping the students' dynamic thinking and organizing them to participate in various kinds of revolutionary practice.[42]

This is a relatively complete inventory of educational reforms carried out during this period. The work load of the students was lightened, teaching methods were reformed, open book examinations were adopted in some universities, and more emphasis was put on ideological education. The statement also reflects a clearer understanding of the Maoist concept of education. Political and ideological education was no longer listed as 'abstract, theoretical learning'.

Activities to improve the quality of education, however, still remained within the confines of the regular schools. The irregular schools were to be consolidated, but reports on what actually took place are few, perhaps again reflecting the ambivalent feelings about these schools. In April 1963, the Ministry of Education called a meeting of the personnel of spare-time schools from the provinces of Fukien, Heilungkiang, Shangtung, Shensi, Szechwan, Kansu, Honan, and Peking at which they were urged to seek the help of related departments in running their schools. The conference was reconvened the following year and the policy was reaffirmed. There are isolated newspaper reports on these schools, but the enthusiasm which characterized such accounts in the early sixties is missing. Perhaps as part of a policy to redistribute the spare-time schools, they were set up in the rural areas. Even so, they appeared to be more like community centres where the educated youth could meet in the evening and carry out some cultural activities.

The same unwarranted enthusiasm that characterized the GLF became manifest again. Cadres often carried the new policies to extremes. As a reaction to the previous emphasis on academic studies, extracurricular activities were now encouraged. By 1965, some students were complaining that they were holding too many responsible positions. During the forty days of summer holidays, they were fully occupied organizing summer camps and inter-school activities, with little time left for rest.[43] These protests led to a cutting down of extracurricular activities in the following year.

Redistribution of Educational Opportunities

To redress the imbalance in the distribution of schools, there was now renewed activity. More work/study schools were set up, mainly in the rural areas:

> According to statistics of 25 provinces, cities, and autonomous regions alone, the number of participants in spare-time education was estimated at more than 10 million. In Shansi province, for instance, 65 hsien and cities have established a total of more than 13,800 winter and privately run schools with a total attendance of some 1,200,000 peasants. In Shangtung, the number of students in the rural sparetime schools has reached more than 1,500,000.[44]

Not only was there an increase in the number of schools in the rural areas, it was reported that they conscientiously adhered to the mass line; as directed, the cadres consulted the lower and middle peasants and the curricula were made relevant to local conditions. They became technical stations where new techniques were disseminated, agricultural experiments were carried out, and where peasants were encouraged to come for advice. By the end of 1965, there were 40 million attending these schools, and their number was on the increase.[45]

Opposition, nevertheless, continued to exist at the implementation level. The work/study agricultural schools were sometimes criticized as unorthodox; newspapers and journals in 1964 and 1965 carried reports of complaints. At the opening of one of these schools, one remarked: 'This school is not what a school should be and this production team is not what a production team should be. ... A school should not serve only the educational needs of the poor and middle peasants.'[46] When the spare-time schools were first established, some elites had arrogantly dismissed the benefits of education for the workers and peasants, saying that: 'Culture is of no use ... in plowing the land and carrying manure. You have no use of trigonometry or geometry; all you need is physical strength'.[47]

Ideological Education
Opposition notwithstanding, the social consciousness of the masses began to change. As the Maoist influence began to prevail, there was a growing public demand to exert pressure on the schools to carry out positive ideological education. The Socialist Education Movement was dedicated to raising the revolutionary zeal of the urban masses. As part of this movement, thousands of high school and university students visited the rural areas to receive their ideological education. In the urban areas, young people were assembled to listen to the old residents: 'In the course of the socialist education movement, the Communist Youth League branch of Miao Street, Hofei, organized youths to listen to street histories from the old residents'.[48] Pressures for ideological education also came from the 'Learn from Lei Feng' and 'Learn from PLA' movements. Students attended exhibitions and slide shows organized by neighbourhood communities; they gathered information on Lei Feng for school projects, and were exhorted to learn from his proletarian spirit. During this period, the works of Mao Tse-tung were also published in large quantities and widely disseminated. Study groups set up to read and discuss his work were especially popular among the peasants and workers, but similar groups could be found in the schools as well. Attempts were made to incorporate Mao's thought into political courses.

In the growing debate within literary and art circles, the influences of the feudal outlook on these subjects came under critical review. This led to closer attention to the reading materials and activities of the children. In the libraries, books with feudal ideas were taken out and replaced with revolutionary stories. Parents and teachers were urged to pay more attention to the games played by their children, and to encourage them to play more wholesome games. Those that emulated kings and nobles and incorporated the old feudal structures were to be discouraged; the guerrillas and revolutionaries of the liberation movement should be the children's heroes.

All these activities no doubt represented a deliberate attempt of the Maoist faction firmly to inculcate its ideology in the schools. However, educational reforms entailing any radical transformation of the existing structure continued to be misunderstood or sabotaged, so that the desired effects of the policies never transpired. It was soon realized that even these measures were not enough to effect the desired changes—the hold of the traditional elites within the educational system was still too strongly entrenched. During this period, attempts to redistribute educational opportunities were thwarted by the policy of 'squatting at a point'. The preoccupation of raising academic standards within the regular schools further polarized the two-track system of education. To effect any real radical changes, the power of the elites had to be broken. The structure of the existing system had to be drastically transformed. This was one of the reasons for the launching of the Cultural Revolution.

PRELUDE TO THE CULTURAL REVOLUTION

Throughout this period, there were raging newspaper debates on art and literature and on the philosophical front, centring on Yang Hsien-chen's theory of 'two combined into one', Teng T'o's concept of morality, and Sun Yeh-Fang's 'balanced economy'. However, the students do not appear to have taken an active part in these comparatively abstract discussions. Their concerns were more with the practical issues that affected their lives.

In 1963, however, the debate on 'happiness' attracted much attention among the students. The discussions turned to a consideration of material incentives and ideological motivation in academic circles. Some held that there was nothing wrong in enjoying the fruits of one's labour. They criticized the opposition view that working for the collective constituted happiness. Another debate centred on class background: Should a person with a landlord background be admitted into the Young Pioneers or Communist Youth League? Was a person with a peasant background automatically 'red'? That is, did a person's material existence determine his ideological outlook? Another debate centred on the question of agricultural work. Some students felt it was a waste of their education to work in the rural areas; others felt it depended on one's ideological perspective. There was also the question of whether students performing productive labour in the rural areas should receive special treatment. Discussions like these reflected a growing consciousness among the students, preparing them for their participation in the Cultural Revolution.[49]

Not all the students were 'red'; many expressed bourgeois thoughts. That this could happen in persons born or educated in the socialist era probably indicates the influence of the surviving capitalist viewpoints of their family and teachers, two important socializing agents in any society. The fact that so many individualistic ideas could be uttered so openly and without recrimination shows that such ideologies were still widespread at this time.

As the struggle escalated in the political arena, students were mobilized by the Maoist faction. The educational system was the first structure to come under attack. Lu Ping, the president of Peking University was criticized for supporting the 'Three Family Village' of Teng T'o, Wu Han, and Liao Mo-sha who were accused of undermining socialism. Teng T'o, as a counter-measure, organized seminars to discuss the play Dismissal of Hai Jui and attempted to limit the criticism to an academic debate. A big wall poster, put up by seven students of Peking University, criticizing the existing enrolment system, demanding drastic reforms, and pledging their support for Mao, received the approbation both of Mao himself and students across the country.

Attempts through the years to sabotage educational reforms now were unmasked. Many of the accused administrators in the universities of Wuhan, Chungshan, Nanking, and Chengchow were dismissed. The editors of Chinese Youth and Chinese Woman were purged. The newspapers, Peking Daily and Frontline, were reorganized. The mayor of Peking, P'eng Chen, was dismissed, and the Municipal Council of Peking was reorganized. Those who were purged in this period were mostly engaged in educational work; they were not just cadres at the implementation level and included many among the decision-makers. P'eng Chen, a member of the Politburo was purged. Kuo Mo-jo, a member of the CCPCC, wrote his self-criticism. In fact, most of the members of the education ministry were later purged during the Cultural Revolution. (See Table 15)

Table 15 Directors and Ministers of Education Criticized or Purged During the Cultural Revolution

		Criticized or Purged	Date
Office of Culture and Education			
Director:	Chang Chi-ch'un	*	Jan. 1967
Deputy Directors:	Chang Chia-fu	—	—
	Hsu Mai-chin	—	—
	Kao Yun-p'ing	—	—
	Chang Meng-hsu	*	Jan. 1967
Ministry of Culture			
Minister:	Lu Ting-i	*	Dec. 1966
Vice-ministers:	Hu Yu-chih	—	—
	Hsu Kuang-hsiao	*	— 1967
	Hsu Ping-yu	*	April 1967
	Liu Pai-yu	*	Feb. 1967
	Shih Hsi-min	*	Jan. 1967
	Yen Chin-sheng	*	April 1967
	Li Chi	*	March 1967
	Lin Mo-han	*	Dec. 1966
	Hsia Wang-tung	*	July 1967
	Chao Hsin-ch'u	*	— 1967
Ministry of Higher Education			
Minister:	Chiang Nan-hsiang	*	Jan. 1967
Vice-ministers:	Liu Yang-chiao	*	Jan. 1967
	Kao Yi	—	—
	Tuan Lo-fu	*	Jan. 1967
	Huang Hsin-pai	—	—
Ministry of Education			
Minister:	Ho Wei	*	Nov. 1966
Vice-ministers:	Liu Chi-ping	*	Jan. 1967
	Liu K'ai-feng	*	June 1968
	Yeh Sheng-t'ao	—	—
	Lin Li-ju	*	Jan. 1967

Source: *Who's Who in Communist China* (Hongkong: Union
Research Institute, 1969).
* : Purged.   — : Information not available.
Note: These offices were promulgated in 1965 after the 3rd NPC. Of
those who held these offices in 1959, Chang Chi-chun, Yang Hsui-
feng, Chien Chun-jui, Hsia Yen, Lin Mo-han, Liu K'ai-feng, and Lin
Li-ju were criticized or purged.

In June, the central government issued regulations to reform admission procedures and postponed all enrolment for half a year.

> Bourgeois domination is still deeply rooted and the struggle between the proletarian and the bourgeois is very acute in quite a number of universities, colleges, and middle schools. The system of examination and enrolment for the institutions of higher learning, though it has been constantly improved since the liberation, has failed in the main to free itself from the stereotype of the bourgeois system of examination. Such a method is harmful to the implementation of the line of education formulated by the Central Committee of the Party and Chairman Mao. ... This system of examination must be completely changed; therefore time is needed to consider and find new methods of enrolment.[50]

The Red Guard first appeared in July, formed by students of institutes of higher learning to carry out revolution within the schools. On August 8, 1966, the government announced 'the Decision Concerning the Great Proletarian Cultural Revolution', in which it was stated that the main object was to purge a 'faction of power holders who followed the capitalist road'. The Cultural Revolution had officially begun.

The struggle began as a debate on the ideological front. The theories of Yang, Sun, and Teng, which provided the rationale for Liu's policies of the early sixties, came under attack. These debates gradually spread to the educational system, dealing at first with fundamental questions about its structure, then growing into an intense power struggle, with criticism, self-criticism, conflict, and later on, physical violence. The political struggle, in essence, represented a concentrated expression of the struggle between the lines of development advocated by Mao and Liu. It is in this perspective that the Cultural Revolution should be viewed. It was not a power struggle per se between two rival leaders. It was an ideological struggle over which road China was to take to become truly socialist. The remnants of the capitalist system had exhibited a resilience which defied change. The Cultural Revolution was designed to break its stranglehold on the emerging socialist society. Should China depend on the common people or on the experts among the bourgeoisie? Should she pursue the goal of raising the level of economic development at the expense of advancement towards socialism? Should she smash the existing structure to make way for a new one? The policies of the early sixties seemed to have reinforced existing capitalist tendencies. Should they be abandoned? As its name implies, the Cultural Revolution was a struggle on the cultural front over which ideology should dominate in a period of transition, the bourgeois or the proletarian?

★9★

Summary and Conclusion

Events in China between 1958 and 1966 offer many insights into the relationship between the economic base and educational development. They tend to confirm, at least in this particular case, certain basic Marxist tenets.

RELATIONSHIP BETWEEN
EDUCATION AND THE SOCIAL MILIEU

The economic substructure is the determinant of educational development. It influences educational development not only through the level of production, which is closely associated with the forces of production, but through the social relationship within the production process and ownership of property.

Ownership of property is the most crucial element: it determines who controls the educational system and whose interest it will serve. In China, property is owned by the state on behalf of the proletariat (workers and peasants). They control the economic base and the state apparatus, including the ideological state apparatus—the educational system. Ultimately we go full circle; the purpose of the educational system of China is to serve the interests of the proletariat, and the ideology of the Communist Party provides the guidelines for educational development.

In 1958, the hegemonic group launched the GLF in an effort to raise the level of production of the country and to equalize the existing differences between the rural and the urban areas, thus moving China closer towards communism. To bring these things about, the emphasis shifted from heavy industry to the simultaneous development of agriculture and industry, and experts were called on to integrate with the proletariat and acquire their outlook.

The educational policies announced in September 1958 were formulated specifically to meet the demands of the GLF: to meet the needs of the rural population, agricultural middle schools were set up in rural areas; the curricula and student activity were especially geared to agricultural needs; the integration of theory with practice, mental with manual labour, was emphasized.

The structure in the economic base was not conducive to the fulfilment of these ideals, however. Private property was redistributed, but vestiges of the social relations of production that existed in the capitalist era survived: the division of labour was still organized on a hierarchical basis, and remuneration was still based on one's position within the hierarchy and one's capabilities, which in turn were largely determined by one's level of education. The ideology that supported private property had not been completely routed. Moreover, within the educational system, the traditional elite controlled the implementation level and continued to represent the interests of the ousted landowning and bourgeois classes in contradiction to the concept of education embodied in the thoughts of Mao Tse-tung. Resenting the idea of restructuring education to meet the needs of the proletariat, many resisted pursuing the policies issued from the centre.

In the years 1960–62, deteriorating economic conditions led to a reassessment of the policies of the GLF. While there was no fundamental change in the class basis of power, there was a turnover within the hegemonic group which showed up as a shift in strategies. The economic policies of China were to continue to serve proletarian interests, but now the simultaneous development of industry and agriculture gave way to an emphasis on agriculture. The mass line was not repudiated, but more attention was paid to planning and coordination, to raising the level of production through a dependence on experts, and to a reliance on material incentives to increase production.

There was a related shift in educational policies. Education was to provide the trained manpower needed to raise the level of development. To meet this requirement, regular schools were improved, scientific research was encouraged, advanced students received special attention, and the work/study schools were consolidated or phased out. A more bureaucratic administrative style replaced mass mobilization in the running of the schools.

The educational and economic policies of the sixties reinforced each other, nurturing the growth of capitalist tendencies, such as the pursuit of profit and widespread speculation in the rural markets. Although the level of production improved, there was a widening gap between the poor and the rich at this time. In education, the academic level was probably raised, but there was an overall drop in enrolment, especially in the rural areas where many schools had been closed down. The peasants, once again, were the main losers.

While economic conditions did improve, recognition of the ramification of the policies of consolidation led to a new balance of power within the hegemonic group around 1963, with some opting for a change of policies. Many of the policies of consolidation were retained; others reminiscent of the GLF were re-instated. However, the educational sector exhibited a greater resistance to change than did the economy. The traditional elite at the implementation level continued to resist attempts to serve proletarian interests; they opposed the policies favouring renewed reliance on the extension of educational opportunities through work/study schools, the integration of theory and practice, manual and mental labour, and the cultivation of 'red and expert' individuals. It soon became apparent that in order to attain these socialist ideals, the power of the traditional elite had to be smashed and the whole educational structure revamped.

Developments in the early sixties showed that the economic base influenced education not through the level or forces of production alone, but through the social and property relations of production. Economic developments not only influenced the educational policies formulated, but also their implementation. They determined who controlled the schools, the content, and organization of the curricula.

Other parts of the superstructure interact with education and shape its development. The formulation of educational policy and its implementation were influenced to a great extent by what was going on in the political superstructure. In China, the hegemonic group within the political system was the Communist Party, which acted as the vanguard of the proletariat in the revolution and as their representative in the existing political structure; but at the implementation level, members of the traditional elites exerted a persisting influence because they had been dominant in the economic base before liberation and had more education, on the whole, than the rest of the population, giving them an initial advantage in the socialist era.

While there were several changes in the strategy of development in the fifties and sixties, there was no fundamental change in the class basis of power. Both the Maoist and the Liuist policies were intended to serve the proletarian interests and to promote communism. The alternating emphases of policy represented, rather, different factions within the hegemonic group, each of which was advocating different strategies for arriving at the same goal.

There were more than two viewpoints within the hegemonic group; a number of different shades of opinion existed. However, the Maoist and Liuist factions were dominant. Shifting lines of support between these two groups swung the balance from Mao to Liu and back again, with each shift being preceded by a period of uneasy balance of power. The workings of these shifting alliances is not a matter of public record; it can only be inferred from the conflicting trends that often coexisted. In late 1958, for example, Mao's resignation was followed by the directive to consolidate existing educational facilities. At the same time, P'eng, who criticized Mao, was also dismissed. The policies of Mao were reaffirmed, but, in effect, they were replaced by the policies of retrenchment. By the mid-sixties, the policy of consolidation itself came under attack. Many top party personnel, including Sun Yeh-fang, Yang Hsien-chen, Chou Yang, and P'eng Chen, were criticized and purged, and those higher up the party echelon were also implicated. The mid-sixties was a period in which, on the one hand, policies of consolidation and retrenchment were implemented and, on the other, the socialist education movement was launched to mobilize the masses.

Educational policies were also affected by the power balance at the implementation level, especially when the centre pointed only to the direction of development, while the allocation of resources and the methods of implementation had to be worked out at the local level. Since the educational system was dominated by the traditional elite, the policies of the GLF did not receive full support from the implementers. Even the masses, who stood most to gain from educational reforms, in general, were suspicious of them. Consequently, at the lower level, the policies of the GLF did not produce the desired effects. This failure, combined with the onslaught of natural disaster, prompted a reassessment of educational priorities. A period of consolidation and retrenchment that was carried out with a greater degree of sympathy and faithfulness because it conformed more with a traditional concept of education, followed.

By the mid-sixties the accumulated effects of the ideological campaign that had never ceased ever since the liberation became more evident. The masses had gained a greater degree of social consciousness and had begun to appreciate the advantages of the work/study schools; the students gradually became more active and critical of weaknesses in the system. This growing support for the Maoist policy of development among the clientele of the educational system began to balance out the support for the Liuist line among the implementers who had been educated in the pre-liberation period, and this shifting power balance at the implementation level in turn affected the balance of power at the hegemonic level. However, the control of the educational system by the traditional elite was still strong, and many, in effect, sabotaged central attempts to gear education to meet proletarian needs. It became increasingly evident that the school system had to be revolutionized before any socialist policy could be successfully carried out.

Events in the other parts of the superstructure also affected educational development, often in contradictory ways. The reallocation of manpower to the rural areas during the anti-waste campaign of 1958, for example, contributed to a great extent to the establishment of the irregular schools. On the other hand, with the emphasis on anti-waste, the original purpose of setting up these schools—the integration of theory with practice and bridging the gap between manual and mental labour—was sometimes lost in the exclusive attention devoted to cutting down state expenses.

Other movements within the ideological superstructure also influenced educational development. Members of the old order had strong control of the educational system, making the implementation of socialist policies difficult. However, ideological campaigns were carried out on a widespread scale and gradually infiltrated the school system. The 'Learn from Lei Feng', 'Learn from PLA', and the 'Study of Mao Tse-tung's Thoughts Campaign' during the mid-sixties, though initiated outside the schools, gradually spread into them.

Each structure has its own dynamics of existence. The educational system is also influenced by its own internal dynamics. An educational system, once started, generates its own dynamics of existence. The legacy of a capitalist-style educational system in China, with its emphasis on academic study and reliance on deference to experts and the examination system, ensured that it would remain within the preserve of the elite. Further, it produced a generation with unquestioning faith in the legitimacy of the existing system and weeded out those who would not abide by or support it.

The interests of the elites thus were served not only in the feudal-capitalist era; the continuing mechanism effectively perpetuated their interests even under changing conditions. When the socialist system superseded the capitalist one, it was no longer acceptable to teach Confucian ideology. But while the content of the curriculum was changed, many of the old structures remained untouched. The examination system continued to emphasize rote learning and supplied society with a generation who conformed to the traditional educational system and its trust in experts. The control of the system remained with the elite, who continued to disseminate their ideology to the younger generation.

When changing policies threatened the status quo, the implementers incorporated the new directives into their teaching, but did so in a manner that protected the basic capitalist ideology they stood for. The memorization of ideological treatises, the continued emphasis on academic achievement, the implementation of policies in a formalistic manner, all rendered the principles of mass mobilization, unity of theory and practice, and the creation of irregular schools largely ineffective and sometimes even ridiculous. In effect, it created a two-track educational system and a new breed of elite, but continued to protect the interests of the rich. Recognizing the resilience of the capitalist structure, the government eventually launched an all-out attempt to change the system.

The economic system also had its own internal dynamics to regenerate itself. However, given the importance attached to the economy, the government made a better coordinated effort to smash the capitalist structure within the system, aiming its efforts at the very foundation of the traditional power base—private ownership. True, many characteristics of the capitalist social relations of production remained, but these were weaker compared to those in education, illustrating the lag in the development of education towards socialism.

Contradictions exist within and between the economic substructure and the educational superstructure. The contradictions inherent in the internal dynamics of a structure are accentuated in a period of transition. In the Chinese socialist economic structure, there were contradictions between technical advances and mass mobilization, urban and rural development, industry and agriculture, heavy and light industry. Contradictions within the educational superstructure were reflected in debates between 'red and expert', quantity and quality, theory and practice, mental and manual labour. However, these contradictions were not antagonistic because they were not mutually exclusive; compromise could be made.

On the other hand, the contradictions between the socialist and the capitalist system were antagonistic and mutually exclusive; each vied with the other for domination in China's economic and educational systems. The economic base had been largely transformed to a socialist one, with property ownership controlled by the state; however, this represented only a technical transformation. The ideology supportive of private ownership, a limited form of private ownership and free trade, and the class divisions based on these capitalist survivals remained, vying with the socialist structure for domination. Within the educational system, because of the limited availability of trained manpower, control at the implementation level remained in the hands of the trained elite. This group resisted any basic change in the structure of the educational system. Although attempts were made to unify theory with practice, mental with manual labour, and to bridge the gap between rural and urban areas, the curricula within the schools remained academic. Theory was divorced from practice; expertise was isolated from 'redness'. Admission procedures and activities within the schools which emphasized individual academic achievement worked against the fulfilment of socialist collective ideals.

Contradictions within China's economic system were especially apparent, since it is the property relationship that basically distinguishes the socialist system from the capitalist one. Collective ownership, ideological motivation, and dependence on the masses are characteristic of the socialist system; private ownership and material incentives are the hallmarks of capitalism. If China was to become a truly socialist society, every effort had to be made to root out the surviving capitalist tendencies.

Contradictions between capitalism and socialism in the educational system also existed, but here they were more subtle, not immediately obvious. As a result, the hegemonic group was sometimes caught off guard. Their intent, for example, to raise academic standards in the sixties, thus increasing the level of production in the socialist economic base, was achieved, but at the expense of the proletariat; the power base of the elite was reinforced, prolonging the existence of capitalist tendencies in the educational system.

The resilience of capitalist characteristics in a period of socialist transition accentuates internal contradictions within a system, sometimes even transforming non-antagonistic contradictions into antagonistic ones. For example, the Liuist strategy of developing heavy industries in the urban areas, which is in itself noncapitalist in intent, accentuated the gap between the workers and the peasants, urban and rural areas, running counter to the socialist ideal of equal distribution. More important, Liu's dependence on technology in the economy and academic achievement in education unwittingly supported the emergence of a new type of elite in the socialist era.

In view of the existence of contradictory tendencies within, and the lag in the rate of development towards socialism between the economic and the educational systems, we would expect contradictions in the relationship between the two systems. The educational system was regarded as the ideological state apparatus for generating socialism within the economic base. What this meant in fact was that educational structures still inherently capitalist were called on to perform functions contradictory to their ideology. For example, when the socialist economic system required the educational system to create a generation of 'red and expert' intellectuals, ready to work for the proletariat, the control of the traditional elite, with its emphases on theory, high academic standards, and admission procedures, worked against this aim. Similar situations also existed within the economic system where capitalist tendencies sometimes conflicted with the socialist educational goal. For example, the economic system offered differential rewards based on expertise, which served to undermine the attractiveness of socialist ideals lauded in the schools.

When capitalist tendencies within the educational system were reinforced, they tended to support similar characteristics in the economic system, thus retarding the movement towards socialism in Chinese society. But when socialist tendencies predominated in the educational system, the transition to socialism in the economic base was accelerated and the capitalist tendencies in both structures were weakened.

Attempts to resolve contradictions constitute the dialectics of the developmental process. During the GLF, there were conflicting emphases on quantity and quality within the educational system. In the haste to universalize education, the quality of the schools was lowered. In using both the regular and irregular schools to universalize education, the regular schools acquired a special status. In emphasizing the unity of theory and practice, mental and manual labour, the schools sometimes became convenient labour pools for communities. The anti-waste campaign in the economic base provided resources to establish rural schools, but sometimes concern with the prevention of waste overshadowed the importance of ideological education.

In the early sixties, the recognition by the hegemonic group of these conflicting emphases resulted in a policy shift. However, this only created new contradictions. To correct the tendency of overstraining the resources, the work/study schools were closed, depriving the poorer sectors of society of educational opportunities. The renewed emphasis on academic pursuits bolstered the positions of the bourgeois intellectuals, strengthened their control of the educational system, and provided the children of the wealthier peasants with better opportunities for schooling. But all these changes worked to the disadvantage of the masses. The continual resurgence of capitalist tendencies within the Chinese educational system, which ran counter to the requirements of the socialist society, was one of the reasons for the launching of the Cultural Revolution.

MEDIATION PROCESS

The economic base, while playing a determinant role in educational development, did not affect it in a mechanistic way: that is, educational development did not react mechanically to changes in the economic structure. The economic substructure exerted an influence on the superstructure through the mediation of its agents. Educational development was the outcome of a complex process of interaction between objective conditions, the ideology of those involved, and their power relations.

One's personal ideology provides the filter through which each of us perceives and interprets objective conditions. In China, the Communist Party, as the holder of power, provided the ideology for the functioning of the state. That of the hegemonic class, as embodied in the thoughts of Mao Tse-tung, provided the overall guidelines for the direction in which the economic and educational systems of China were to move: the central purpose of the educational system was to support the socialist economic substructure.

However, within the confines of the hegemonic ideology, there were differences of opinion. Even though they all agreed on the principle of the advancement of China towards communism, not all opted for the same strategies of development. This can be seen in the differences between Mao and P'eng Te-huai in the late fifties and the struggle between Mao and Liu in the sixties. In the late fifties, Mao's policy of the GLF represented an impatience to industrialize China quickly. P'eng and Mao disagreed on both the rate of development and the role the masses should play in developing the country. In the sixties, Liu and Mao again reacted differently to the changing conditions. They disputed the relative importance to be put on the forces of production and on mass mobilization. The Liuists emphasized the importance of organization and the use of experts in raising the level of production; the Maoists, on the other hand, put their faith in mass mobilization as the means of overcoming objective difficulties. Consequently, the Liuists favoured closing the agricultural schools to release the manpower for agricultural work and concentrating on the development of regular schools and technical education, while the Maoists opted for the further development of the agricultural schools through mass mobilization, and gave high priority to ideological education.

Differences between the policy-makers and the implementers were even greater. The actual control of policy implementation was largely in the hands of the bourgeois elements of society, educated in the pre-liberation period and steeped in its ideology. They favoured an elitist system of education which concentrated on the training of highly skilled experts.

In the late fifties, when educational policies were aimed at serving the needs of the socialist economic base, stressing the unity of theory and practice, manual and mental labour, and urban and rural areas, many implementers strongly disapproved of the intent behind these policies. They reacted with a mechanical adherence only to the guidelines, meeting the pressure from the centre with hasty implementation and apparent enthusiasm. The consequent establishment of a large number of work/study schools strained local resources and the over-emphasis on the work aspect led to these schools being looked on as convenient labour pools. Not surprisingly, the eventual result was the failure of these schools.

In the sixties, the policies of the GLF were, to a certain extent, blamed for the deteriorating economic conditions. The ensuing power struggle within the hegemonic group finally led to the domination of the Liuist strategy of development. To correct the tendency of spreading the resources too thinly and too hastily, a policy of consolidation and retrenchment was adopted. To counter the lowered academic standards resulting from the proliferation of part-time schools, academic reform was emphasized and existing schools were consolidated. Since these policies were more in line with the implementers' perceptions of education, there is little evidence of opposition to this change in direction. On the contrary the reports of the time point to enthusiastic efforts to raise the standards of the regular schools.

The renewed emphasis on academic standards again gave power and prestige to the intellectuals and provided their children with more opportunities to distinguish themselves. The difference in status between the graduates of the regular and irregular schools further widened. Graduates of the regular schools were much influenced by the capitalist ideologies and offers of material rewards for achievement. Many were unwilling to work in collectives or in rural areas after they were trained.

In the mid-sixties, the recognition of the capitalist ideology within the predominantly socialist framework, tendencies that ran counter to socialist ideals, led to a struggle at the decision-making level to reverse the policies of retrenchment and consolidation. With the concurrent rise in the political consciousness of the masses, there was a similar struggle between the clientele and the implementers. These struggles finally merged with the Cultural Revolution, whose central purpose was to eradicate all remnants of the influence of the capitalist economic system in China.

EDUCATIONAL DEVELOPMENT 1958–66 AND THE EDUCATIONAL ASPECT OF THE CULTURAL REVOLUTION

The educational innovations introduced during the Cultural Revolution are often regarded as radical breaks from earlier times. However, many of the changes were not as new as they may first appear. For example, the system of 'three in one'—the participation of the teachers, students, and workers in the administration of the educational system—instituted after the Cultural Revolution, was in line with Mao's idea of mass line. He had tried to put it into practice as early as the Yenan Period and on a nation-wide scale in 1958, when he called for the mobilization of the masses in establishing their own schools. Neither was the cancellation of the examination system in the universities and the adoption of open book examinations something new. This had already been tried out in the early sixties. In the method of selection after the Cultural Revolution, high school graduates were expected to do agricultural work for two years, and were then recommended to enter universities by their fellow workers. The earlier policy of 'from the commune and back to the commune' had been patterned on the same philosophy. Members of the communes were to recommend qualified persons to undertake training and to return to their locality to work after graduation.

The basic difference between the educational reforms in the late fifties and early sixties and those of the Cultural Revolution was perhaps in the degree of implementation. In the early period, many of the reforms received great opposition or token approval only, resulting in a large number never getting off the ground. With the Cultural Revolution, there was a direct attack on the holders of power in the educational system. Now that the masses had attained a higher degree of political consciousness and had been transformed into an active collectivity, they joined with the centre in ousting the traditional elites from their position of dominance at the implementation level and gained real control of the schools through the 'three in one' method of administration. The success of the Cultural Revolution paved the way for the smoother implementation of educational reform in the interest of the proletariat.

It must be emphasized that the reforms of the Cultural Revolution were the culmination of developments in the previous decade. The repeated failure to reform the educational system made the hegemonic group realize that it needed to smash the entire structure before a new edifice could be built. A new communist educational system could not be superimposed on old structures; a more radical and basic transformation was required before socialist policies could work.

Reforms in the preceding decades also culminated in the development of the Cultural Revolution in another sense. The educational reforms and ideological campaigns carried out in the fifties and early sixties had helped to transform a passive collectivity into a relatively active one, allowing a radical transfer of power. These educational reforms, though unsuccessful in many respects, had pointed out to the masses the direction that should be taken. Now that they had gained a greater degree of control, even at the implementation level, educational reforms that served the class interest of the proletariat could be widely adopted. However, one must realize that ideological transformation is a long drawn-out process. Resistance would still be present, not only among the traditional elites, but among the masses also. Opposition would occur, there would still be conflict and contradictions.

OUTCOME OF EDUCATIONAL DEVELOPMENT

To what extent was the educational system supportive of the growth of the socialist economy in China in its first decades? Statistics on educational development after 1960 are scarce, but the following offer some impressions of her achievements up to 1966.

Judging from the growth of her educational facilities, great strides had been made in the provision of education for the masses. Enrolment in the elementary schools by 1966 had more than trebled, compared with the pre-liberation period. The rate of increase was even greater at the secondary level, where it increased twelve times, and at the university level, where it increased eight times. Even by a conservative estimate, the percentage of children attending schools was probably over 80 percent, though it rapidly decreased higher up the educational scale. Despite the spectacular increases at the higher levels, only one in ten attending primary school could go to secondary school, and one in a hundred in the secondary school could receive a university education.

Educational opportunities were also more equally distributed than in the pre-liberation period, though inequality still persisted. The gap between rural and urban areas was to a certain extent bridged by the work/study schools, but these schools were mainly at the primary and secondary levels, and universities were still concentrated in the urban areas, especially in the eastern region.

By mid-1960, it was estimated that about 40 percent of the students in universities were from the worker-peasant background. Their percentage was even higher further down the educational scale; however, it remained a fact that the children of the rich peasants and the professional class were able to take greater advantage of education than were those of the workers and the poorer peasants. And among the latter group, the workers had a greater advantage than the peasants, judging from the distribution of the schools.

The number of graduates at each level is not available, making it impossible to estimate the dropout rate. It is also hard to estimate whether the number of graduates met the manpower needs of the economy. However, it is not the quantity of graduates alone that is important. Their level of skills and their ideological outlook are equally important in any system that wishes to further economic development.

**Table 16 Student Enrolment 1949–65
(Numbers in Thousands)**

School Year	Primary	Secondary (General and Technical)	University
1949–50	24,391	1,268	117
1954–55	51,218	4,195	253
1959–60	90,000	12,000	810
1964–65	80,000	12,500	—

Note: 1949, 1954 figures are taken from *Ten Great Years* (Peking: Foreign Languages Press, 1960), p. 192; 1959, 1964 figures are from Jan S. Prybyla, *The Political Economy of Communist China* (Scranton: International Textbook Company, 1970), p. 449.

In China, at this time, there was growing recognition within both regular and irregular schools of the need to gear the curriculum to local needs. University students spent some time each academic year in acquiring the proletarian outlook through actual field experience, and graduation theses tended to have a practical rather than a theoretical orientation. At the primary and secondary levels of the regular schools, the curricula appeared to be more academically oriented than in the agricultural schools, where the courses catered to the particular needs of the economy. In the latter schools, there were courses on production skills with the emphasis on local conditions, the use of the abacus was taught in mathematics classes, and the writing of contracts in the language classes. There was considerable regional variation in the extent to which these schools put policy into practice, but the extent to which their graduates were appreciated by the peasants indicates that curricula were meeting local needs.

Caution should be used in interpreting the role of education in the ideological transformation of the young. In theory, there were to be political courses taught at all levels and in all kinds of schools with the aim of studying party documents and the thoughts of Marx, Lenin, Mao, and acquiring the proletarian outlook and the necessary skill to analyse the current national and international situation. However, in many cases, these courses became merely another academic exercise and were confined to learning political theories by rote. The acquisition of an outlook actively supportive of the socialist economic base was not seriously pursued. One of the signs of the failure of ideological education was the unwillingness of many graduates to work in outlying areas.

To a certain extent, education had produced positive results. The population at large had a better chance to obtain an education, their cultural level had been raised, they had become less apathetic. The peasant's traditional fear of government officials now began to give way to criticism of existing policies and the corrupt practices of some officials. The students were the first to question existing educational structures and to criticize administrators and intellectuals, the traditional embodiment of authority. The growing activism of all these groups was a testimony to the achievements education had made in raising the cultural level and the political consciousness of the masses.

CONCLUSION

The development of education in China during the years 1958–66 and its relationship to the economic substructure amply demonstrates the applicability of the Marxist perspective in capturing the reality of a society in transition—the determining role of the economic structure and the contradictions that accompany the process of development. The economic base influences education not only through the forces of production, but also through its property and social relations.

What has been done in this study is to extend the Marxist tenets to an analysis of the mediation process between the economy and the educational superstructure. At the policy-making level, the hegemonic group represents the interests of the dominant class in the economic base. The economic policies formulated result from the hegemonic group's views on economic needs and the balance of power among its members. The educational policies formulated result from the policy-makers' view on how to meet these economic needs. How faithfully these policies are carried out by the implementers depends on their commitment to the hegemonic ideology and the power balance at the implementation level. Objective conditions, in turn, affect the outcome of educational development.

Educational development is a product of the interaction of several influences: objective conditions, the ideology of the hegemonic group, the power balance among the hegemonic group, the ideology of the implementers, and the power balance at this level. Events in China between 1949 and 1966 confirm Poulantzas' argument that the hegemonic group is not a homogeneous one; different shades of opinion are present which sometimes result in intense power struggles. However, they also reveal that Poulantzas' concept of the bureaucracy as a pliant tool of the hegemonic group is not applicable, at least to a society in transition. When there is a radical transformation in the economic base, the bureaucracy, which is made up of the ousted traditional elites, is antagonistic to the ideology of the hegemonic class and, when given the opportunity, they may subvert policies and try to reinstate the former system.

Events during this period provide deeper insights into the educational development of a society in transition. They put in perspective the crucial role played by the autonomy and the supportive or contradictory roles of other parts of the superstructure. The adoption of every policy and its implementation was accompanied by struggle and conflict among and between the policy-makers and the implementers, dispelling the concept of China as a totalitarian country with a monolithic power structure.

Developments in this period also provide the background to the Cultural Revolution. It was not born, full-grown, overnight. Rather, it represents the culmination of a continuing struggle between two opposing strategies for socialist development: the Maoist and the Liuist lines. Beginning as an attempt to break with the capitalist past, it became predominantly an ideological struggle to eradicate the remnants of capitalist tendencies in the society.

The radical educational reforms of the Cultural Revolution do not represent any sudden break with the past. They are the cumulative product of a long and tortuous process of educational reform that extended over nearly two decades. The traditional elites' strong control on the educational system foiled many previous attempts to rid it of lingering capitalist tendencies. What occurred with the Cultural Revolution was a direct attempt to oust the traditional elites from their position of power at the implementation level. The subsequent turnover of power to the masses made way for more radical reforms.

To both analysts and practitioners of social change, this study demonstrates the tremendously important role played by the implementers. It points to the fallacy of overlooking the mediation process, of focusing exclusively on policy and its outcome, and of trying to explain the failure of policies in terms of objective conditions alone. It also points to the importance of looking at the level of economic development as well as at the property and social relations of production. Finally, it points to the dilemmas inherent in any attempt to implement change in a period of transition. On the one hand, the contribution of the traditional elites cannot be ignored. On the other hand, basic change cannot be accomplished by superimposing piecemeal changes on existing structures; it requires radical attack, aimed at their very foundations.

APPENDIX ★ I

Abbreviations Used in Text

CCP   Chinese Communist Party
CCPCC   Chinese Communist Party Central Committee
FFYP   First Five Year Plan
GLF   Great Leap Forward
KMT   Kuomingtang (Nationalist Party)
NPC   National People's Congress
PLA   People's Liberation Army
SC   State Council
SFYP   Second Five Year Plan

Abbreviations Used in Notes

CB   *Current Background*
ECMM   *Extracts from China Mainland Magazines*
NCNA   New China News Agency
SCMM   *Selections from China Mainland Magazines*
SCMP   *Survey of China Mainland Press*

APPENDIX ★ II

Changing Alliances within
the Hegemonic Group
1958–1966

Period 1

Mao-Liu Group[a]
Chiang Nan-hsiang
K'ang Sheng
K'o Ch'ing-Shih
Liu Shao-ch'i
Lu Ting-i
Mao Tse-tung
Po I-po
T'an Chen-lin
T'ao Chu
Ulanfu

Supporters of SFYP
Ch'en Yun
Chou En-lai
Teng Tzu-hui

P'eng Group[b]
Chang Chung-liang
Chou Hsiao-chou
P'eng Te-huai

Period 2 and 3

Mao Group
K'ang Sheng
Lin Piao
Mao Tse-tung
Yao Wen-yuan

Liu Group[c]
Ch'en Yi
Chou Yang
Kuo Mo-jo
Lin Mo-han
Liu Shao-ch'i
Lu Ting-i
P'eng Chen
Sun Yeh-fang
Teng Hsiao-p'ing
Teng T'o
Wang Jen-chung
Wu Han
Yang Hsien-chen

(a)   The grouping of individuals is based on statements made by them in the mass media.
(b)   *The Case of Peng Teh-huai* (Hongkong: Union Research Institute, 1968).
(c)   This list is derived from the purges that took place during the period.

APPENDIX ★ III

Key Names and their Chinese Translation

Chang Chi-ch'un	張際春	Lin Mo-han	林默涵
Chang Chia-fu	張稼夫	Lin Piao	林彪
Chang Chih-chung	張治中	Liu Chi-p'ing	劉季平
Chang Chung-liang	張仲良	Liu K'ai-feng	劉瞪風
Chang Meng-hsu	張孟旭	Liu Pai-yu	劉白羽
Chao Hsin-ch'u	趙辛初	Liu Shao-ch'i	劉少奇
Ch'en K'e-han	陳克寒	Liu Tzu-tsai	劉子載
Ch'en Yi	陳毅	Liu Yang-ch'iao	劉仰嶠
Ch'en Yun	陳雲	Lu Ting-i	陸定一
Chiang Nan-hsiang	蔣南翔	Mao Tse-tung	毛澤東
Ch'ien Chun-jui	錢俊瑞	P'eng Te-huai	彭德懷
Chou En-lai	周恩來	Po I-po	薄一波
Chou Hsiao-chou	周小舟	Shen Yen-ping	沈雁冰
Chou Yang	周楊	Shih Hsi-min	石西民
Fan Ch'ang-chiang	范長江	Sun Yeh-fang	孫冶方
Hsia Yen	夏衍	T'an Chen-lin	譚震林
Hsiao Wang-tung	蕭望東	T'ao Chu	陶鑄
Hsu Kuang-hsiao	徐光霄	Teng Hsiao-p'ing	鄧小平
Hsu Mai-chin	徐邁進	Teng T'o	鄧拓
Hsu P'ing-yu	徐平羽	Tuan Lo-fu	段洛夫
Hu Yu-chih	胡愈之	Ulanfu	烏蘭夫
Huang Hsin-pai	黃辛白	Wang Jen-chung	王任重
K'ang Sheng	康生	Wu Han	吳晗
Kao Yi	高沂	Yang Hsien-chen	楊獻珍
Kao Yun-p'ing	高雲屏	Yang Hsiu-feng	楊秀峰
K'o Ch'ing-shih	高慶施	Yao Wen-yuan	姚文元
Kuo Mo-jo	郭沫若	Yeh Sheng-t'ao	葉聖陶
Li Ch'i	李琦	Yen Chin-sheng	顏金生
Lin Li-ju	林礪儒		

★ NOTES ★

Chapter One

1. K. E. Priestley, *Education in China*; R. F. Price, *Education in Communist China*; David Milton, 'China's Long March to Universal Education', *Urban Review* 5 (May 1972): 3–9. Some of the exceptions are Marianne Bastid, 'Economic Necessity and Political Ideals in the Educational Reform during the Cultural Revolution', *China Quarterly* 42 (July 1970): 16–45; Stewart Fraser and John N. Hawkins, 'Chinese Education: Revolution and Development', *Phi Delta Kappan* LII (August 1972): 487–500; Theodore Ch'en, *The Maoist Educational Revolution*.
2. For example, W. Taylor, *The Secondary Modern School* (London: Faber & Faber, 1963); D. V. Glass, 'Education and Social Change in Modern England', in A. H. Halsey et al, eds., *Education, Economy and Society* (Glencoe: Free Press, 1961).
3. For example, O. Banks, *The Sociology of Education* (London: Batsford Ltd., 1969).
4. B. Barber, 'Resistance by Scientists to Scientific Discovery', in W. J. Chambliss, ed., *Sociological Readings in the Conflict Perspective* (Reading: Addison Wesley Publishing Co., 1973), p. 2.
5. Karl Marx, *Critique of Political Economy*, pp. 20–21.
6. Ibid.
7. Engels' letter to J. Bloch, in *Karl Marx and Frederick Engels, Selected Correspondence*, p. 475.
8. Louis Althusser, *For Marx*, p. 101.
9. Karl Marx and Frederick Engels, 'Manifesto of the Communist Party', in L. S. Feuer, ed., *Basic Writings on Politics and Philosophy*, p. 7.
10. Karl Marx, *Capital* (New York: International Press, 1967), I: 568.
11. Louis Althusser, *Lenin and Philosophy*, pp. 121–73.
12. Martin Carnoy, *Education as Cultural Imperialism*.
13. David McLellan, *Marx's Grundrisse* (St. Albans: Paladin, 1971), p. 126.
14. Henri Lefebvre, *The Survival of Capitalism: Reproduction of the Relations of Production* (New York: St. Martin's Press, 1976).
15. Nicos Poulantzas, *Political Power and Social Class*, pp. 70–72.

186 Notes to pages 11–27

16. Nicos Poulantzas, *Fascism and Dictatorship*.
17. The term 'capitalist' will be used to describe Chinese society before 1949, and the word 'socialist' to denote the period after that. These two words will also be used to delineate characteristics of the pre-liberation and the post-liberation periods respectively. I will also term any policy or measure that helped to 'reproduce' the characteristics of the pre-liberation period as capitalist and those that tried to institutionalize the ideology of the new hegemonic group as socialist. They are used in place of others like pragmatism versus idealism or slower versus faster rate of growth because these latter terms concentrate on the strategies of development whereas the former carry with them much deeper social meanings and put the different approaches to development in a much broader historical perspective.
18. V. I. Lenin, *The State and Revolution*; Ralph Miliband, *The State in Capitalist Society*; Poulantzas, *Political Power and Social Class*.
19. Lenin, *The State and Revolution*, p. 8.
20. Poulantzas, *Political Power and Social Class*, p. 339.
21. Nicos Poulantzas, 'On Social Class', *New Left Review*, 78 (April 1973): 27–54.
22. Ralph Miliband, *The State in Capitalist Society*.
23. Karl Marx, *Critique of Political Economy*, p. 21.
24. Ibid.
25. Quoted from John Gurley, *China's Economy and the Maoist Strategy*, p. 204.
26. For example, Parris H. Chang, *Power and Policy in China* (University Park: Pennsylvania State University Press, 1975); Robert A. Scalapino, ed., *Elites in the People's Republic of China*.

Chapter Two

1. Audrey Donnithorne, *China's Economic System*, chap. 1.
2. *Collected Works of Liu Shao-ch'i 1958–1967*, p. 5.
3. Ibid., p. 58.
4. 'Adhere to the Method of Class Analysis, Correctly Understand the Struggle Between the Two Lines', *Red Flag* 13 (December 1971), in *SCMM*, no. 719 (December 1971), p. 18.
5. John Lewis, *Leadership in Communist China*, p. 110.
6. Liu Shao-ch'i, *How to Be A Good Communist*, p. 56.
7. Franz Schurmann, *Ideology and Organization in Communist China*, p. 33.
8. John Lewis, *Leadership in Communist China*, p. 108.
9. Sidney Leonard Greenblatt, 'Organizational Elites and Social Change at Peking University', in Robert A. Scalapino, ed., *Elites in the People's Republic of China*, pp. 451–500.
10. Mao Tse-tung, 'On Correcting Mistaken Ideas in the Party', *Selected Works*, 1: 112.

11. *Directory of Chinese Communist Officials* (U.S. Government, 1966); *Who's Who in Communist China* (Hongkong: Union Research Institute, 1966). The Ministry of Higher Education was abolished for a brief period during The Great Leap Forward.
12. A. Doak Barnett, *Cadres, Bureaucracy, and Political Power*, p. 19.
13. *Who's Who in Communist China.*
14. Mao Tse-tung, 'On the Correct Handling of Contradictions Among the People', *Selected Readings from the Works of Mao Tse-tung* (Peking: Foreign Languages Press, 1971), p. 459.
15. Peter R. Moody, Jr., *The Politics of the Eighth Central Committee of the Chinese Communist Party.*
16. Mao Tse-tung, 'On Contradictions', *Selected Works*, 1: 336.
17. Mao Tse-tung, 'On the Correct Handling of Contradictions Among the People'; Liu Shao-ch'i, *On Inner Party Struggle* (Peking: People's Press, 1950), pp. 32–33. For further details on the ideological differences between the two leaders, see Lowell Dittmer, *Liu Shao-ch'i*, pp. 31–67; A. E. Kent, *Indictment Without Trial*; and Cheng Yung Ping, *Chinese Political Thought, Mao Tse-tung and Liu Shao Ch'i* (The Hague: M. Njihoff, 1966).
18. Liu, in 1957, said that class struggle had in the main ended (*People's Daily*, August 26, 1967, in *SCMP* 5012, pp. 21–25) whereas Mao asserted that class struggle was by no means over (*People's Daily*, November 26, 1967, in *SCMP* 4071, pp. 18–27).
19. For example, *P'an t'u nei chien kung tsei Liu Shao Ch'i ti tsui cheng* [Evidence of the Crimes of Liu Shao Ch'i, the traitor, spy, and public enemy] (Hongkong: Contemporary Chinese Research Institute, 1968), and 'Liu Shao Ch'i shi kan t'ai tsui' [The Ten Crimes of Liu Shao Ch'i] in *Liu Shao Ch'i Wen T'i Tsu Liao Chuan Chi* [special volume on Liu Shao Ch'i] (Chung Kung Yen Chui Tsa Chin She, 1970) [Communist China Research Publishing Co.], p. 373.
20. For further explanation as to how the traditional elites stood to benefit from Liu's policy, see pages 37–38.
21. For details of changes in the administrative structure over the years, see D. J. Waller, *The Government and Politics of Communist China* (London: Hutchinson University Library, 1970), chap. 5.
22. *People's Daily*, January 18, 1958, in *SCMP* 1705, p. 21.
23. Mao Tse-tung, 'Proletarian Dictatorship and Renegade China's Kruschev', August 1967, in *CB* 885, p. 34.

Chapter Three

1. *Three Major Struggles on China's Philosophical Front* (Peking: Foreign Languages Press, 1973).
2. John N. Hawkins, *Mao Tse-tung and Education.*
3. Karl Marx, *Critique of Political Economy*, pp. 20–21.
4. Jerome Ch'en, *Mao.*

5. For details, see Peter Seybolt, 'The Yenan Revolution in Mass Education', *China Quarterly* 48 (October 1971): 641–70; Mark Selden, *The Yenan Way*.
6. Mao Tse-tung, 'On New Democracy', January 1940, *Selected Works*, 2: 340.
7. Mao Tse-tung, 'Talks on the Yenan Forum', May 1942, ibid., 3: 86.
8. Mao Tse-tung, 'On the Correct Handling of Contradictions Among the People', *Selected Readings*, 459.
9. Mao Tse-tung, 'Instructions on the Question of Redness and Expertness', CB 891, p. 28, in John N. Hawkins, *Mao Tse-tung and Education*, p. 71.
10. Mao Tse-tung, 'Report to the Executive Central Committee of the Chinese Soviet Republic', 1934, *Chinese Education* 1 (April 10, 1970), p. 35.
11. Mao Tse-tung, 'Policies, Measures, Perspectives for Resisting the Japanese Invasion', July 1937, *Selected Works*, 2: 18.
12. Mao Tse-tung, 'On the Correct Handling of Contradictions Among the People', *Selected Readings*, p. 459.
13. Mao Tse-tung, 'Proletarian Dictatorship and Renegade China's Kruschev', August 1967, CB 885, p. 34.
14. Mao Tse-tung, 'Rectify the Party's Style of Work', 1942, *Selected Works*, 3: 39.
15. Mao Tse-tung, 'On Contradictions', August 1937, ibid., 1: 336.
16. Mao Tse-tung, 'On Practice', July 1937, ibid., 1: 295–310.
17. Mao Tse-tung, 'A Study of Physical Education', in Stuart R. Schram, ed., *The Political Thought of Mao Tse-tung*, p. 94.
18. Mao Tse-tung, 'Talk at the Hangchow Conference', December 1965, in Stuart R. Schram, ed., *Mao Unrehearsed*, p. 336.
19. Mao Tse-tung, 'Reform our Study', May 1974, *Selected Works*, 3: 20.
20. Mao Tse-tung, 'Rectify the Party's Style of Work', February 1942, ibid., 3: 39.
21. Ibid., p. 40.
22. Mao Tse-tung, 'On New Democracy', December 1939, ibid., 2: 381.
23. Mao Tse-tung, 'Instructions on the Question of Consolidating Anti-Japanese Military and Political College', CB 897, p. 10.
24. John N. Hawkins, *Mao Tse-tung and Education*, p. 100.
25. Mao Tse-tung, 'Speech at the CCP's National Conference on Propaganda Work', CB 888, p. 7.
26. Mao Tse-tung, 'Remarks at the Spring Festival, February 1964', in Stuart R. Schram, ed., *Mao Unrehearsed*, p. 205.
27. John N. Hawkins, *Mao Tse-tung and Education*, p. 104.
28. Mao Tse-tung, 'Resolutions of the Ninth Congress of the Fourth Army of the Red Army of the CCP, 1929', CB 888, p. 12.
29. Mao Tse-tung, 'Remarks at the Spring Festival, February 1964', in Stuart R. Schram, *Mao Unrehearsed*, pp. 204–5.

30. Ibid.
31. 'Border Region Government Directive, 1943', quoted in John N. Hawkins, *Mao Tse-tung and Education*, p. 88.
32. Ibid.
33. Mao Tse-tung, 'Concerning Methods of Leadership', June 1943, *Selected Works*, 3: 118–19.
34. Mao Tse-tung, 'Talk with the Nepalese Educational Delegation on Education Problems, 1964', *CB* 891, p. 50.
35. Mao Tse-tung, 'Rectify the Party Style of Work', February 1942, *Selected Works*, 3: 35–52.

Chapter Four

1. Kuan Ta-tung, *The Socialist Transformation of Capitalist Industries and Commerce in China* (Peking: Foreign Languages Press, 1960), p. 35.
2. Audrey Donnithorne, *China's Economic System*, p. 146; 'Industries', in *Communist China 1949–1959*, p. 154.
3. Kuan Ta-tung, *The Socialist Transformation*, p. 35.
4. John G. Gurley, *China's Economy and the Maoist Strategy*, p. 125.
5. Stephen Andors, *China's Industrial Revolution*, p. 55.
6. Christopher Howe, *Wage Patterns and Wage Policy in Modern China, 1919–1972*, pp. 31–34.
7. Hsueh Mu-ch'iao, *The Socialist Transformation of the National Economy in China* (Peking: Foreign Languages Press, 1960), p. 91.
8. William Hinton, *Fanshen*; C. K. Yang, *The Chinese Family in the Communist Revolution*.
9. Hsueh Mu-ch'iao, *The Socialist Transformation*, p. 87.
10. John G. Gurley, *China's Economy and the Maoist Strategy*, p. 213.
11. Audrey Donnithorne, *China's Economic System*, pp. 38–43.
12. Leo A. Orleans, *Professional Manpower and Education in China*, p. 71.
13. Carl Riskin, 'Small Industries and the Chinese Model of Development', *China Quarterly* 46 (April 1971): 245–73.
14. The income differential between the industrially advanced and backward areas was 1.66:1 and that between the urban and rural areas was 2:1. See Christopher Howe, *Wage Patterns and Wage Policy*, chap. 2, for further details.
15. Audrey Donnithorne, *China's Economic System*, p. 38.
16. Hsueh Mu-ch'iao, *The Socialist Transformation*, p. 93.
17. Jan S. Prybyla, *The Political Economy of Communist China*, p. 184.
18. Hsueh Mu-ch'iao, *The Socialist Transformation*, p. 9.
19. Alexander Eckstein, 'Economic Growth and Change in China', *China Quarterly* 53 (January 1973): 211–41.
20. Stephen Andors, *China's Industrial Revolution*, p. 55; Christopher Howe, *Wage Patterns and Wage Policy*, p. 36.

Chapter Five

1. Hu Shi-Ming and Eli Seifman, *Toward a New World Outlook* (New York: AMS Press, 1976), pp. 3–4.
2. Chinese Ministry of Education, 'The Second Chinese Education Yearbook', in Tsang Chiu-sam, *Society, Schools and Progress in China*, p. 192.
3. Leo A. Orleans, *Professional Manpower and Education in China*, pp. 14, 15, and *Ten Great Years*, p. 192.
4. 'Speech made by the Minister of Education, Mr. Ma Hsu-lun, at the Conference on Higher Education on June 1, 1950', *People's Daily*, June 14, 1950, p. 1.
5. NCNA, July 21, 1951, in *SCMP* 142, pp. 5–12.
6. *Peking Review* I (December 1958), p. 16.
7. 'Speech made by the Minister of Education, Mr. Ma Hsu-lun, at the Conference on Higher Education on June 1, 1950', *People's Daily*, June 14, 1950, p. 1.
8. *Students' Directory of Higher Education* (pamphlet), Peking Ministry of Higher Education, 1958, in Leo A. Orleans, *Professional Manpower and Education in China*, p. 57.
9. NCNA, February, 1954, in *SCMP* 747, pp. 27–29.
10. See Hu Shi-Ming and Eli Seifman, *Towards a New World Outlook*, pp. 1–84.
11. *People's Daily*, October 3, 1951, p. 1.
12. NCNA, February 1, 1954 in *SCMP* 747, pp. 27–29.
13. Tsang Chiu-sam, *Society, Schools and Progress*, pp. 167–68.
14. Leo A. Orleans, *Professional Manpower and Education in China*, pp. 14–15.
15. *People's Daily*, August 3, 1950, p. 3.
16. Tsang Chiu-sam, *Society, Schools and Progress*, p. 167.
17. *Wen Hui Pao* [Literary Gazette], February 26, 1955, in *SCMP* 1067 (Supplement no. 1071), pp. 8–9 and *Kuang-ming Daily*, June 18, 1955, in *SCMP* 1094, pp. 16–17.
18. For details of these campaigns, see Gordon Bennett, *Yundong: Mass Campaigns in Chinese Communist Leadership* (Berkeley: Center for Chinese Studies, 1976); Charles P. Cell, 'Making the Revolution Work: Mass Mobilization Campaigns in the People's Republic of China', Ph.D. dissertation, University of Michigan, 1973.

Chapter Six

1. *Eighth National Congress of the Communist Party of China*, 3 vols. (Peking: Foreign Languages Press, 1956), I: 232.
2. *Sixth Plenary Session of the Eighth Central Committee of the Communist Party of China* (Peking: Foreign Languages Press, 1958), p. 5.
3. Cheng Chu-yuan, *The Economy of Communist China 1949–1969* (Ann Arbor: Michigan Papers in Chinese Studies, 1971), p. 3.

4. Mao Tse-tung's speech in Moscow, quoted in F. Schurmann, *Ideology and Organization*, p. 199.
5. *Sixth Plenary Session of the Eighth Central Committee of the Communist Party in China* (Peking: Foreign Languages Press, 1958), p. 5; CKCNP [Chinese Youth Newspaper], October 17, 1958, in *SCMP* 1904, p. 13.
6. *Eighth National Congress of the Communist Party of China*, 3 vols. (Peking: Foreign Languages Press, 1956), I: 248.
7. Ibid., II: 176.
8. Ibid., II: 314.
9. Roderick MacFarquhar, *The Hundred Flowers Campaign and the Chinese Intellectuals* (New York: Praeger, 1960), p. 57.
10. *Hsin-hua Pan Yueh Kan* [New China Half-monthly Magazine], 3 (1951), from *Communist China* (Hongkong: Union Research Institute, 1960), p. 121.
11. *Collected Works of Liu Shao-chi 1958–1967* (Hongkong: Union Research Institute, 1968), p. 14.
12. Peter R. Moody, Jr., *The Politics of the Eighth Central Committee of the Chinese Communist Party*, p. 128.
13. See Chou En-lai's speech, quoted in *Eighth National Congress of the Communist Party of China*, I: 261–328.
14. *Red Flag* 1 (January 1959), pp. 6–11.
15. NCNA, December 29, 1958, in *SCMP* 1920, p. 16; NCNA, January 21, 1959, in *SCMP* 1942, p. 3.
16. NCNA, June 25, 1958, in *SCMP* 1807, p. 10.
17. Franz Schurmann, *Ideology and Organization in Communist China*, p. 475.
18. *People's Daily*, September 19, 1958 in *SCMP* 1833, p. 12.
19. Ibid., p. 12.
20. Ibid., p. 12.
21. NCNA, May 26, 1958, in *SCMP* 1869, p. 7.
22. *Kuang-ming Daily*, September 4, 1958, in *SCMP* 1869, p. 3.
23. *People's Daily*, March 23, 1958, in *SCMP* 1747, p. 3.
24. CKCN [Chinese Youth], 13 (July 1958), in *ECMM* 143, p. 31.
25. *Chiao Shih-pao* [Teachers' Newspaper], July 1, 1958, in *SCMP* 1814, p. 9.
26. CKCN [Chinese Youth], May 13, 1958.
27. *Kuang-ming Daily*, July 15, 1958, in *SCMP* 1831, p. 15.
28. *Hsueh hsi* [Learning], 15 (August 1958), in *ECMM* 146, p. 26.
29. *People's Daily*, March 10, 1959, in *SCMP* 1985, p. 16.
30. NCNA, August 1958, in *SCMP* 1847, p. 12.
31. NCNA, June 4, 1958, in *SCMP* 1788, p. 20.
32. NCNA, March 20, 1959, in *SCMP* 1985, p. 14.
33. NCNA, August 25, 1958, in *SCMP* 1847, p. 11.
34. NCNA, April 14, 1959, in *CB* 558, p. 1.
35. *CSKS* [China's Handbook of Politics and Economy], 1965, p. 385.

36. *Kuang-ming Daily*, June 10, 1958, in *SCMP* 1814, p. 46; NCNA, July 9, 1958, in *SCMP* 1814, p. 47; NCNA, October 29, 1958, in *SCMP* 1888, p. 14; NCNA, April 14, 1959, in *CB* 558, p. 1.
37. *CSKS* [China's Handbook of Politics and Economy], 1965, pp. 382–85.
38. *Ten Great Years* (Peking: Foreign Languages Press, 1960), p. 201.
39. NCNA, December 19, 1957, in *SCMP* 1683, p. 11.

Chapter Seven

1. Jan S. Prybyla, *The Political Economy of Communist China* p. 271.
2. Anna Louise Strong, *The Rise of the Chinese People's Commune and Six Years After* p. 113.
3. Ibid., p. 120.
4. *Sixth Plenary Session of Eighth CCPCC* (Peking: Foreign Languages Press, 1958), p. 50.
5. Audrey Donnithorne, *China's Economic System*, p. 85; *Red Flag* 2 (January 1959), p. 10.
6. *The Case of Peng Teh-huai*, p. 24.
7. Ibid., p. 11.
8. Peter Moody, *The Politics of the Eighth CCPCC*, p. 141.
9. 'Ten Crimes of Liu Shao-ch'i', December 29, 1966, in *Liu Shao Ch'i Wen T'i Tzu Liao Chuan chi* [Collection of material on Liu Shao-ch'i] (Chung Kung Yen Chiu Tsa Chin She, 1970) [Communist China Research Publishing Co.] p. 373.
10. L. Dittmer, *Liu Shao-ch'i and the Chinese Cultural Revolution*, p. 41.
11. Mao Tse-tung, 'On Contradictions', *People's Daily*, April 10, 1960.
12. NCNA, March 30, 1960, in *CB* 615, pp. 1–25.
13. NCNA, September 28, 1962, in *CB* 691, p. 1.
14. Ibid., p. 1.
15. *Nanfang Daily*, April 7, 1962, in *SCMP* 2750, p. 4.
16. Ibid., p. 4.
17. NCNA, April 6, 1960, in *CB* 616, p. 18.
18. L. Dittmer, *Liu Shao-ch'i and the Chinese Cultural Revolution*, pp. 247, 257.
19. The allegation that Liu Shao-ch'i was responsible for this policy is often based on his statement in 1962 that, 'Industry must retreat to a sufficient extent and so must agriculture, by fixing quotas based on the household and allowing individual farming'. For example, see *People's Daily*, August 28, 1967, in *SCMP* 4021, pp. 9–14. In the early sixties, there was no news report of Liu making any statement to this effect.
20. Audrey Donnithorne, *China's Economic System*, p. 46.
21. L. Dittmer, *Liu Shao-ch'i and the Chinese Cultural Revolution*, p. 250.

22. NCNA, April 8, 1960, in CB 691, p. 1.
23. Ibid., p. 16.
24. Jen Min Chiao Yu [People's Education], February 1960, in SCMP 2212, p. 121.
25. NCNA, April 9, 1960, in CB 623, p. 4.
26. Ibid., p. 4.
27. Peter Moody, The Politics of the Eighth CCPCC, p. 152.
28. NCNA, January 24, 1962, in SCMP 2671, p. 13; NCNA, November 17, 1961, in SCMP 2629, p. 25 and People's Daily, May 18, 1960, in SCMP 2275, p. 11.
29. People's Daily, May 15, 1962, in SCMP 2753, p. 11.
30. Kuang-ming Daily, July 8, 1962, in SCMP 2786, p. 18.
31. Chung-Kuo Ching-nien Pao [Chinese Youth Newspaper], August 13, 1960, in CB 640, p. 8.
32. Kuang-ming Daily, July 17, 1960, in CB 640, p. 1.
33. Kuang-ming Daily, October 25, 1962, in SCMP 2849, p. 8.
34. Kuang-ming Daily, July 23, 1962, in SCMP 2799, p. 6; People's Daily, July 13, 1960, in SCMP 2301, p. 21.
35. Kuang-ming Daily, July 9, 1960, in SCMP 2314, p. 17.
36. NCNA, March 10, 1960, in CB 615, p. 20.
37. NCNA, March 10, 1960, in SCMP 2218, p. 10; NCNA, July 1, 1960, in SCMP 2294, p. 18.
38. NCNA, April 7, 1960, in SCMP 2240, p. 14.
39. Nanfang Daily, February 15, 1962, in SCMP 2703, p. 6.
40. Kuang-ming Daily, July 23, 1962, in SCMP 2799, p. 25.
41. Kuang-ming Daily, March 3, 1962, in SCMP 2703, p. 7.
42. Stephen Andors, China's Industrial Revolution, p. 128.

Chapter Eight

1. NCNA, January 17, 1963, in SCMP 2916, p. 10.
2. China Reconstructs 4 (April 1965), ECMM 465, p. 36; Peking Review 40 (October 1963), in ECMM 387, p. 35.
3. NCNA, December 31, 1965, in SCMP 3611, p. 23.
4. People's Daily, March 8, 1965, in SCMP 3423, p. 7.
5. Ta Kung Pao [newspaper], February 20, 1965, in SCMP 3412, p. 9.
6. In an address to a group of graduates Liu even encouraged them to strive for upward mobility. See L. Dittmer, Liu Shao-ch'i and the Cultural Revolution, p. 251.
7. Peter Moody, The Politics of the Eighth CCPCC, p. 155.
8. NCNA, September 28, 1962, in CB 691, p. 1.
9. Mao Tse-tung, Selected Readings, p. 503.
10. L. Dittmer, Liu Shao-ch'i and the Chinese Cultural Revolution, chap. 5.
11. See Red Flag 16 (August 1964); People's Daily, August 14, 1964, in

SCMP 3296, pp. 1–10; *People's Daily* July 17, 1964, in SCMP 3294, pp. 1–7.

12. *People's Daily*, June 21, 1966, in SCMP 3732, p. 10.
13. *Peking Review* 41 (October 1963), in ECMM 388, p. 20.
14. *Kuang-ming Daily*, January 21, 1963, in SCMP 2925, p. 1.
15. *People's Daily*, December 1963, in SCMP 3117, p. 7.
16. *Peking Review* 40 (October 1963) in ECMM 387, p. 35.
17. *People's Daily*, March 24, 1963, in SCMP 2953, p. 2.
18. *People's Daily*, February 5, 1966, in SCMP 3642, p. 6.
19. *Yang-cheng Evening News*, July 7, 1966, in SCMP 3744, p. 1, and *People's Daily*, February 20, 1965, in SCMP 3416, p. 1.
20. *People's Daily*, December 2, 1963, in SCMP 3771, p. 11.
21. NCNA, December 1, 1963, in SCMP 3117, p. 6 and *Kuang-ming Daily*, December 3, 1963, in SCMP 3132, p. 13.
22. Ibid.
23. *People's Daily*, December 4, 1965, in SCMP 3599, p. 11.
24. *People's Daily*, March 27, 1963, in SCMP 2959, p. 5.
25. *People's Daily*, March 25, 1963, in SCMP 3209, p. 2.
26. *People's Daily*, December 4, 1965, in SCMP 3599, p. 11.
27. *People's Daily*, March 25, 1964, in SCMP 3209, p. 2.
28. 'A talk in Hangchow', in Jerome Ch'en, ed., *Mao Papers* (London: Oxford University Press, 1970), pp. 105–7.
29. *People's Daily*, September 6, 1965, in SCMP 3543, p. 21.
30. *Kuang-ming Daily*, April 19, 1966, in SCMP 3689, p. 15.
31. *People's Daily*, March 25, 1964, in SCMP 3209, p. 2.
32. *People's Daily*, July 13, 1965, in SCMP 3515, p. 3.
33. L. Dittmer, *Liu Shao-ch'i and the Chinese Cultural Revolution*, p. 272.
34. *Kuang-ming Daily*, March 7, 1964, in SCMP 3190, p. 8.
35. NCNA, May 6, 1963, in SCMP 2977, p. 15.
36. *Yang-cheng Evening News*, July 12, 1966, in SCMP 3734, p. 12.
37. *Kuang-ming Daily*, July 11, 1965 in SCMP 3507, p. 6.
38. *Yang-cheng Evening News*, July 12, 1966, in SCMP 3743, p. 12.
39. *People's Daily*, July 19, 1966, in SCMP 3751, p. 13.
40. *Shanghai Education*, 7 (July 1965), in ECMM 492, p. 5.
41. *Nanfang Daily*, March 25, 1963, in SCMP 2973, p. 32.
42. NCNA, January 6, 1964, in SCMP 3150, p. 4.
43. *Yang-cheng Evening News*, August 22, 1965, in SCMP 3539, p. 11.
44. *People's Daily*, July 19, 1966, in SCMP 3751, p. 13.
45. *People's Daily*, December 9, 1965, in L. Dittmer, *Liu Shao-ch'i and the Chinese Cultural Revolution*, p. 277.
46. *Nanfang Daily*, September 17, 1964, in SCMP 3327, p. 10.
47. CKCN [Chinese Youth], January 1965, in ECMM 459, p. 33.
48. CKCNP [Chinese Youth Newspaper], November 7, 1963, in SCMP 3115, p. 6.
49. *Nanfang Daily*, November 7, 1963, in SCMP 385, p. 13; CKCNP

[Chinese Youth Newspaper], March 29, 1963, in *SCMP* 2968, p. 11;
CKCNP [Chinese Youth Newspaper], April 21, 1964, in *SCMP* 3226,
p. 8; *CKCNP* [Chinese Youth Newspaper], May 4, 1964, in *SCMP*
3227, p. 14.
50. NCNA, June 18, 1966, in *SCMP* 3724, p. 2.

SUGGESTED ★ READINGS

1. Books and Articles

Althusser, Louis. *For Marx*. New York: Vintage Books, 1969.

———— *Lenin and Philosophy*. London: New Left Books, 1971.

Althusser, Louis and Etienne Balibar. *Reading Capital*. London: New Left Books, 1968.

Andors, Stephen. *China's Industrial Revolution*. New York: Pantheon, 1977.

Barendsen, R. *Half-Work Half-Study Schools in China*. Washington: U.S. Department of Health, Education and Welfare, 1964.

Barnett, A. Doak. *Cadres, Bureaucracy and Political Power in Communist China*. New York: Columbia University Press, 1967.

———— *Chinese Communist Politics in Action*. Seattle: University of Washington Press, 1969.

———— *Uncertain Passage: China's Transition to the Post-Mao Era*. Washington: Brookings Institution, 1974.

Baum, Richard. 'Liu Shao-ch'i and the Cadre Question.' *Asian Survey* 8 (April 1968): 323–45.

Baum, Richard and Frederick C. Teiwes. *Ssu-Ch'ing: The Socialist Education Movement of 1962–1966*. Berkeley: Center for Chinese Studies, 1968.

Bettelheim, Charles, *Cultural Revolution and Industrial Organization in China*. New York: Monthly Review Press, 1974.

Carnoy, Martin. *Education as Cultural Imperialism*. New York: David McKay, 1974.

The Case of Peng Teh-huai. Hongkong: Union Research Institute, 1968.

CCP Documents of the Great Proletarian Cultural Revolution 1966–1967. Hongkong: Union Research Institute, 1968.

Ch'en, Jerome. *Mao*. Englewood Cliffs: Prentice Hall, 1969.

Ch'en, Theodore. *The Maoist Educational Revolution*. New York: Praeger, 1974.

Cheng, Chu-yuan. *The Economy of Communist China*. Michigan Papers in Chinese Studies, 1971.

Cheng, H. *Higher Education in China*. Hongkong: Union Research Institute, 1972.

Cohen, Lenard J. and Jane P. Shapiro. *Communist Systems in Comparative Perspective*. Garden City: Anchor Books, 1974.

Collier, John and Elsie Collier. *China's Socialist Revolution*. New York: Monthly Review Press, 1974.

Communist China 1949–1959. Hongkong: Union Research Institute, 1961.

Dittmer, Lowell. *Liu Shao-ch'i and the Chinese Cultural Revolution: The Politics of Mass Criticism*. Berkeley: University of California Press, 1974.

Donnithorne, Audrey. *China's Economic System*. London: George Allen and Unwin Ltd., 1967.

Eckstein, Alexander. 'Economic Growth and Change in China.' *China Quarterly* 53 (January 1973): 211–41.

Eighth National Congress of the CCP. 3 vols. Peking: Foreign Languages Press, 1956.

Falkenheim, Victor Carl. 'Provincial Administration in Fukien 1949–1966', Ph.D. dissertation, Columbia University, 1972.

Feuer, L. S., ed. *Karl Marx, Basic Writings on Politics and Philosophy*. New York: Anchor Books, 1969.

Fraser, Stewart E., ed. *Education and Communism in China*. London: Pall Mall, 1971.

Gamberg, Ruth. *Red and Expert*. New York: Schocken, 1977.

Goldman, Merle. 'The Fall of Chou Yang.' *China Quarterly* 27 (July 1966): 132–48.

Gramsci, Antonio. *Selections from the Prison Notebooks*. London: Lawrence and Wishart, 1971.

Gurley, John. *China's Economy and the Maoist Strategy*. New York: Monthly Review Press, 1976.

Hawkins, John N. *Educational Theory in the People's Republic of China*. Hawaii: University of Hawaii Press, 1971.

——— *Mao Tse-tung and Education*. Hamden: Linnet Books, 1974.

Hinton, William. *Fanshen*. New York: Monthly Review Press, 1966.

Hoffmann, Charles. *The Chinese Worker*. Albany: State University of New York Press, 1974.

Howe, Christopher. *Employment and Economic Growth in Urban China 1949–1957*. Cambridge: Cambridge University Press, 1971.

———— *Wage Patterns and Wage Policy in Modern China 1919–1972*. Cambridge: Cambridge University Press, 1973.

Hsu Kai-Yu. *Chou En-Lai: China's Gray Eminence*. New York: Doubleday, 1968.

Hu, Chang-Tu. *Chinese Education Under Communism*. New York: Teachers College, Columbia University, 1962.

Kent, A. E. *Indictment Without Trial*. Working Paper No. 2, Department of International Relations, Canberra: Australian National University, 1969.

Lenin, V. I. *The State and Revolution*. Moscow: Progress Publications, 1972.

Lewis, John Wilson. *Leadership in Communist China*. Ithaca: Cornell University Press, 1963.

Lindbeck, John M. H. *China, Management of a Revolutionary Society*. Seattle: University of Washington Press, 1971.

———— *Understanding China*. New York: Praeger, 1971.

Lippit, Victor D. 'Land Reform and Economic Development.' *Chinese Economic Studies*, 7 (1974).

Liu Shao-ch'i. *How to Be a Good Communist*. Peking: Foreign Languages Press, 1964.

———— *Collected Works of Liu Shao-ch'i 1958–1967*. Hongkong: Union Research Institute, 1968.

Mao Tse-tung. *Selected Works of Mao Tse-tung*. 4 vols. Peking: Foreign Languages Press, 1967.

———— *Four Essays on Philosophy*. Peking: Foreign Languages Press, 1968.

Marx, Karl. *A Contribution to the Critique of Political Economy*. London: Lawrence and Wishart, 1971.

———— *The German Ideology*. New York: International Publishers, 1970.

———— *Grundrisse*. New York: Random House, 1973.

Marx, Karl and Frederick Engels. *Selected Correspondence*. New York: International Publications, 1942.

Miliband, Ralph. *The State in Capitalist Society*. London: Quartet Books Ltd., 1973.

Milton, David and Nancy Milton, eds. *People's China*. New York: Vintage Books, 1974.

Moody, Peter R., Jr. *The Politics of the Eighth CCPCC*. Hamden: Shoe String Press Inc., 1973.

Nee, Victor and James Peck. *China's Uninterrupted Revolution*. New York: Pantheon Books, 1973.

Oksenberg, Michael, et al. *The Cultural Revolution: 1967 in Review*. Michigan Papers in Chinese Studies No. 2, 1968.

Orleans, Leo A. *Professional Manpower and Education in Communist China*. Washington: National Science Foundation, 1960.

———— *Every Fifth Child*. Stanford: Stanford University Press, 1972.

Poulantzas, Nicos. *Fascism and Dictatorship*. London: New Left Books, 1974.

———— *Political Power and Social Class*. London: New Left Books, 1973.

Price, R. F. *Education in Communist China*. New York: Praeger, 1970.

Priestley, K. E. *Education in China*. Hongkong: Dragon Fly Books, 1961.

Prybyla, Jan S. *The Political Economy of Communist China*. Scranton: International Textbook Co., 1970.

Richman, Barry M. *Industrial Society in Communist China*. New York: Vintage Books, 1969.

Riskin, Carl. 'Small Industry and the Chinese Model of Development.' *China Quarterly* 46 (April 1971): 245–73.

Robson, William A. and Bernard Crick. *China in Transition*. Beverly Hills: Sage Publications, 1975.

Scalapino, Robert A., ed. *Elites in the People's Republic of China*. Seattle: University of Washington Press, 1972.

Schram, Stuart, ed. *Authority, Participation and Cultural Change in China*. Cambridge: Cambridge University Press, 1973.

———— *Mao Tse-tung Unrehearsed*. Harmondsworth: Penguin Books, 1974.

———— *The Political Thought of Mao Tse-tung*. New York: Praeger, 1965.

Schurmann, Franz. *Ideology and Organization in Communist China*. Berkeley: University of California Press, 1968.

Selden, Mark. *The Yenan Way in Revolutionary China.* Cambridge: Harvard University Press, 1971.

Seybolt, Peter. *Revolutionary Education in China.* White Plains: International Arts and Sciences Press, 1973.

———— 'The Yenan Revolution in Mass Education.' *China Quarterly* 48 (October 1971): 641–69.

Sixth Plenary Session of the Eighth CCPCC. Peking: Foreign Languages Press, 1958.

Strong, Anna Louise. *The Rise of the Chinese People's Communes.* Peking: New World Press, 1964.

Sweezy, Paul and Charles Bettelheim. *On the Transition to Socialism.* New York: Monthly Review Press, 1971.

Ten Great Years. Peking: Foreign Languages Press, 1960.

Three Major Struggles on China's Philosophical Front. Peking: Foreign Languages Press, 1973.

Tsang Chiu-sam. *Society, Schools and Progress in China.* Oxford: Pergamon Press, 1968.

Who's Who in Communist China. Hongkong: Union Research Institute, 1969.

Yang, C. K. *The Chinese Family in the Communist Revolution.* Cambridge: M.I.T. Press, 1959.

2. Periodicals and Annuals

Asian Survey
China Quarterly
China Reconstructs
Current Scene
Chugoku Nenkan (China Yearbook, later known as *New China Yearbook*)
Chugoku Seiji Keizai Soran (China's Handbook of Politics and Economy)
Communist China
Far East Economic Review
Hung-ch'i (Red Flag)
Issues and Studies
Jen-min Chiao-yu (People's Education)
Jenmin Shouts'e (People's Handbook)

Journal of Asian Studies
Peking Review
Shih-shih Shouts'e (News Handbook)

3. Newspapers

Jen-min Jih-pao (People's Daily)
Kuang-ming Jih-pao (Kuang-ming Daily)

4. Collections of Chinese Newspapers and Journals

Chinese Education
Current Background
Extracts of China Mainland Magazines
Joint Publications Research Service
Red Guards Publications
Selections from China Mainland Magazines
Survey of China Mainland Press

★ INDEX ★